BIBLICAL
WOMEN
in the
MIDRASH

BIBLICAL
WOMEN
in the
MIDRASH

A SOURCEBOOK

Naomi Mara Hyman

JASON ARONSON INC.
Northvale, New Jersey
London

First Jason Aronson Inc. softcover edition—1998

This book was set in 11 pt. Goudy by Alabama Book Composition of Deatsville, Alabama.

Library of Congress Cataloging-in-Publication Data

Biblical Women in the Midrash : a sourcebook / [edited by] Naomi M. Hyman.
    p. cm.
  Includes bibliographical references and index.
  ISBN 1-56821-950-4 (hardcover)
  ISBN 0-7657-6030-4 (softcover)
  1. Women in rabbinical literature. 2. Women in the Bible. 3. Midrash—History and criticism. 4. Aggada—Commentaries. I. Hyman, Naomi M.
  BM509.W7B53 1997
  296.1'406'082—dc20

                                    96-38362

Manufactured in the United States of America. Jason Aronson Inc. offers books and cassettes. For information and catalog write to Jason Aronson Inc., 230 Livingston Street, Northvale, New Jersey 07647.

In memory of my grandparents,
Myer Norman and Deborah Rachel Berman,
who taught me that Godwrestling is
part struggle and part embrace

CONTENTS

ACKNOWLEDGMENTS

Six years ago, I began a journey that has led me in the most unexpected, yet familiar, directions. This project, in many ways, is the synthesis of my travels to date. There have been many people along the way who have both challenged and supported me, and their insights have found their way into these pages. Without them, I would still be wandering in the dark.

My parents, Anne and Bernie Zvirman, created a strong Jewish environment—both in our home and in the synagogue they helped to found. In that setting, I grew the deep roots of attachment to Judaism that ultimately pulled me back home.

My husband, Bob Hyman, has been unfailingly supportive of me. The path I have taken is not the one he expected, and he has borne the challenges with great patience and understanding. There are not words enough to express my gratitude and love. Melissa and Alison, my extraordinary step-daughters, have been the source of much joy and growth, opening my mind to the insights of feminism and reopening my heart to the possibility of faith. They have enriched my life immeasurably.

I am grateful to my teachers and colleagues at Gratz College, especially Drs. Marsha Bryan Edelman, Rela Mintz Geffen, and Ruth Sandberg. In addition to sharing with me the best of their respective fields, they have shared with me themselves, and in doing so taught me much about what it means to be a Jewish woman. I would also like to thank the staff of the college's Tuttleman Library, whose patient assistance is much appreciated.

Rabbi Gaylia R. Rooks, Rabbi Judith Z. Abrams, Dr. Simcha Paull Raphael, Dr. Janie T. Levis, and Tom Price have been faithful guides throughout the journey. Without them, this anthology could never have come to fruition.

The Temple in Louisville, Kentucky, has been the fertile field in which this project was conceived and developed. The professional staff have been unfailingly supportive and helpful and have provided me with many opportunities to test my ideas. They have also given me unlimited access to both the public and private libraries of the institution.

I also want to thank the women of The Temple. Their unquenchable thirst for Torah has provided the inspiration for this anthology. I especially want to thank the Wednesday-morning Torah study group, Susan Jaffe, Patty Marks, Laural Reinhart, Sheila Tasman, and Janie Lerner, for helping me to structure this book. As the Rabbis teach, from my students I learned the most.

Roberta Clark, Rabbi Joe Rooks Rapport, Dr. Ruth Sandberg, and Anne Zvirman all read the manuscript and offered helpful and insightful comments. Thanks to each of them. Thanks also to Arthur Waskow for helping me to find the words for the dedication.

Arthur Kurzweil of Jason Aronson Inc. took a chance on me, and I am grateful for the opportunity. I would also like to extend my thanks to Steve Palmé. He and many others at Jason Aronson have endured with great patience the endless questions of a first-time editor. Any errors or omissions are mine alone.

I am particularly grateful to the many women who have contributed their work to this anthology. They are pioneers in this field, and it is my prayer that this book will help to bring them the recognition they deserve. Special thanks to Zeise Wild Wolf and Naomi Graetz for helping to give shape to the entire project.

Finally, and most importantly, I am grateful to the Holy One, Blessed Be, who has indeed kept me alive, sustained me, and brought me to this season.

NAOMI MARA HYMAN
August 1996

INTRODUCTION

I

As an adult, I returned to Judaism. I found in myself an urgent call to do something Jewish, but my vocabulary of words and deeds had never progressed beyond adolescence. I began to study.

I started at the beginning. I studied Torah, Midrash, Talmud. I drank in everything. I marveled at the rabbinic view of God and the world, at a tradition that could preserve in its sacred texts the image of God, lonely in heaven, creating the leviathan as a pet, and playing with it at the end of the day. I ached with the rabbis as they mourned the loss of the Temple, envisioning God's presence, the Shekhinah, departing slowly from her place among us. I began to appreciate the intricacies of the Talmud's arguments and to find God in the middle of a dispute over a garment. I began to know those ancient rabbis and to love and respect them.

This was a far different Judaism than the one I had encountered as a child and abandoned as a young adult. In all fairness to those religious school teachers of mine who gave far more than they got in return, I was now looking through the eyes of an adult. I was also investing many more hours and much more of myself in my studies. However, there was also a qualitative difference in what I encountered. Religious school sought to give us a basic religious indoctrination and the barest minimum of synagogue skills. The texts I now read sought to teach a way of seeing the world and of acting in it.

They showed me something else as well, something I never expected: myself. There I was in all my human imperfection, struggling to figure it out: I was there with the rabbis, questioning the meaning of existence and whether it, perhaps, would have been better had we not been created at all; I was there with Moses, fighting authority and ultimately accepting it; I was there with Jonah, digging deep into myself and discovering emotional baggage; I was there with Esther, struggling with the conflicting loyalties of the assimilated Jew. Very little that troubled or challenged me was absent from the tradition. Moreover, the answers were as real as the questions from my all-too-real world. Comfort came, not from the guidance that the sources offered (although that was there as well), but from the knowledge that there is nothing new under the sun. Study was like a late-night talk with the best and most trusted of friends, where the process of sharing is as important as any advice that is offered.

In my last semester of graduate school, I began studying a second tractate of Talmud, *Ketubot*. The material was troubling to me. *Ketubot* considers the laws of marriage, and in many respects, it understands marriage as a transfer of property. For the most part, I was able to put the material in context for myself, to see it as a product of an earlier time. Then I read the following, concerning a child less than three years old: "[If] a grown-up man has intercourse with a little girl, it is nothing, for [when she is] less than this, *it is as if one puts a finger in an eye*" (Babylonian Talmud, *Ketubot*, 11b, Steinsaltz translation, my emphasis).[1]

I knew that the Sages meant that the act had no halachic (legal) significance with regard to marriage and that such actions were un-equivocally condemned by them. However, I also knew that I was encountering a worldview profoundly different than mine. I could imagine no context in which I or any other woman could make a statement like that. The only possible response I could imagine to the rape of a baby would be to provide care and protection for the child and to find and punish the perpetrator. I would denounce such an atrocity in no uncertain terms—and I would *never* let a statement like this go unchallenged. Where I would have expected outcry, there was only silence. I was not included except as object, as Other. I began to understand the deeper implications of a male-defined tradition.

Suzannah Heschel describes the implications of my struggle this way:

Feminism's central insight contends . . . that our most basic understand-ings of human nature are drawn primarily from men's experiences. A

---

1. It is important to note that the Talmud also discusses sexual relations between an adult woman and a boy under the age of nine. Here, too, the act is seen as having no halachic significance, and there is no direct condemnation of such acts. Babylonian Talmud, *Ketubot*, 11a–11b.

patriarchal outlook begins by making men's experiences normative, equating the human with the male. Not only are women excluded from the process of shaping the outlook, but women's experiences are projected as something external, "other" to that norm. [2]

No matter how hard I studied those texts, I now understood, I would never find my own voice, my own experience in them except perhaps vicariously. I felt betrayed.

Despite my anger, it never occurred to me to turn my back on Judaism or the texts themselves, even though I had done so before for far less compelling reasons. For one thing, there remained the fact that much of what I had studied was not only not offensive, but profoundly moving, even life-transforming. To abandon what transcended gender *because of* gender would be senseless. However, something had irrevocably changed, and I needed to come to terms with it.

Think of your relationship to Judaism like a relationship with a lover, a wise friend suggested. Sometimes there are disagreements, serious ones—but if the connection is strong, you stay with it. You teach one another about the ways in which you experience the world. You learn to see the world through each other's eyes.

Traditional Jewish sources see the world through male eyes. Men have determined what is important because they have defined our culture—and they have given us only part of the picture. Women experience the world differently: not inaccurately, not less clearly, but simply differently. A Judaism that includes women's experience will be a more complete Judaism. When we learn to see the world through the eyes of tradition and when tradition takes into itself women's views of the world, both will grow.

This will not be an easy task. There are many obstacles for women, not least of which is learning the language of our tradition so that we can create our place in it. By this I do not mean Hebrew or Aramaic (although a mastery of these languages is essential for serious study). Rather, I refer to the stories, images, symbols, and even the syntax that are the foundation of the Jewish worldview. One can only acquire this

---

2. Suzannah Heschel. "Introduction," in *On Being a Jewish Feminist*, ed. Suzannah Heschel (New York: Schocken Books, 1983), p. xxi.

knowledge through direct study of the traditional texts themselves, and accessing those sources can be challenging.

In many Orthodox communities, women are unable to study freely because of legal constraints and the demands of an observant lifestyle. Even if a woman were to attain sufficient learning to be considered an authority, her participation in legal matters would be restricted, as would the contexts in which she could teach.

Liberal Jewish women (and men) face a different constraint. Many liberal Jews, particularly of my generation, received a meager Jewish education. Our education generally focused on "synagogue skills" rather than preparation for lifelong study. For us, confronting traditional texts without even the most basic tools is very intimidating.

The body of literature referred to here as traditional texts or classic sources includes many works compiled over thousands of years. Although a substantial portion of it has been translated into English, most of it is accessible only in Hebrew or Aramaic. Even in English, study is challenging. The language of Mishnah, Gemara, and Midrash is a kind of shorthand that assumes a lot of basic knowledge, especially about the Bible. It sometimes seems as if you are reading class notes from a course you did not take.

It is, however, worth the effort. All the criticism of Judaism for being patriarchal, however legitimate, tends to focus attention on what is wrong rather than what is right. There is so much gold to be mined. When we refrain from digging because the task is hard or because some of what we might mine is worthless or even dangerous, we prevent ourselves from ever even seeing the gold. We must learn to encounter the texts head-on because they will sustain us as Jews.

II

Judaism has always understood its written texts to be fluid. That is not to say that there are not "official" versions of the Bible or Talmud, for example. Although the classic texts of Judaism began first as oral traditions, authoritative versions were ultimately edited and set down, and these are no longer subject to change. It is the meaning of these texts that remains fluid. Even in the Talmud, the primary legal document of

Judaism, it is not uncommon to find two conflicting opinions standing side by side. A volume of Talmud is itself an illustration of this fluidity. At the center of the page is a section of the Mishnah (the earliest legal compendium derived from the Torah). Directly after this is the Gemara, which is the commentary on the Mishnah. Typically, the Gemara is considerably longer than the Mishnah and continues for several pages, with the Mishnah and Gemara always occupying the center of the page. The Mishnah and the Gemara together are the Talmud, but there is much more on the page. Surrounding the Talmud text in the center are additional commentaries. At the end of the volume can be found other interpretations that did not fit on the page. It is as if you were sharing a textbook with your classmates, and each of you made margin notes in succession. Each successive reader would have, not only the basic text, but the notes and comments from each of her classmates.

That which is true concerning the halachah is all the more so true for Midrash. The rabbis tell us that this was God's intention from the very beginning. According to tradition, there were really two *Torot* (the Hebrew plural of Torah) given at Mount Sinai: the Written Torah in its fixed state, and the Oral Torah, which would be uncovered via study and interpretation over time. Some hold that the Torah was written in black fire on white fire, and that the white spaces around the black letters hold meanings that we have yet to uncover.

It has also been said, more recently, that we have received only half of the Torah, because the Torah as we know it was written by men and the women's Torah has yet to be revealed. I like to think that the women's Torah can be found in the white fire, in the white spaces whose meanings we have yet to uncover, and that a part of each of our souls is still standing at Sinai, ready to receive it.

This is not to say that the Torah we have before us—the Torah of the black fire—is to be dismissed or disregarded. Whether you consider this Torah to be revelation, the history of the Jewish people, our central myth, or some combination of these, the Torah is still the bones of our people. It is the way we have understood ourselves, the foundation of languages, the supporting structure of our civilization. To abandon it is to abandon Judaism.

There is a lot of room, though, between rejection and unquestioning acceptance. That is where many of us find ourselves. We may question certain assumptions within Judaism: for example, the assumption that the male is normative. We nonetheless continue to struggle for a place within Judaism. The struggle takes place on many fronts. Some grapple with issues of egalitarianism in Jewish communal life. Some search for a spiritual path that they find lacking in synagogue life. Others grapple with the halachic system. In each case, we are struggling to find a place for ourselves within Judaism. Sometimes, that means creating a new one.

Midrash has, in many respects, been the way in which Jews have attempted to put themselves and the issues of the times into the ancient story. Classic midrashim (the plural of *midrash*) address an enormous range of topics, finding a source for each in Torah. Midrash was (and is) a way of filling in the "missing pieces" of the biblical narrative, of praising God and taking God to task, of challenging enemies, and of reflecting on what it means to be a Jew. The process of midrash not only offers contemporary Jews an authentic way of making the text our own, but also provides a precedent for such activity. This is an important point for many of us who have been taught not to tamper with tradition. Making midrash is not only an acceptable activity, it is a sacred one.

Jews of today write midrash for the same reason our ancestors did: It is our prayer, our plea, and our affirmation. It is the way we insist that our voices be heard while at the same time giving honor to a tradition that has sustained us even as it pushed us aside. We write because we want our children to have stories that are both Jewish and feminist. We write because in the writing, we find places for ourselves in the white spaces between the black letters.

III

This book is intended as a starting point. It has three objectives. The first is to teach basic text-study skills and to encourage further study. The second is to compare and contrast the way in which traditional rabbinic sources and modern feminists understand the same topic: women of the Bible. The final goal is to introduce the voices of some of these contemporary women commentators with the hope and prayer that their ideas will become part of the language of Judaism.

The first section of the book is designed to provide a basic introduction to the classic Jewish texts included in this volume and to provide some guidelines on how to use the anthology. The chapter, "An Introduction to Bible," provides an overview of the Bible: what is included and how it has been studied. "An Introduction to Midrash" attempts to explain this genre and to suggest the ways in which it has been understood. It also addresses the question of whether contemporary interpretations can rightly be called Midrash. "How to Study" presents some options for individual, partner, and group study, as well as some suggestions as to how to approach the texts themselves.

The second part of this book is an anthology of biblical narratives, selections from the body of work known as Midrash, and contemporary women's interpretations, all on the women of the Bible. Each chapter is dedicated to a woman, or to two women when their lives and stories are intertwined. All of the chapters include material from each of the three sources, so that readers can follow the course of the interpretations. I have excerpted the biblical material in order to create coherent narratives focused on the women. The contemporary material varies greatly, and includes essays, poems, and stories.

All quotations from the Bible, except those cited as part of the rabbinic midrashim or unless otherwise noted, are from the Jewish Publication Society's *TaNaKH*, published in 1985. Talmudic references are from the Soncino Press edition of *The Talmud* (1935–1952), again unless otherwise noted. I have intentionally chosen to quote readily available English sources rather than write original translations. It is my hope that in doing so, readers will become comfortable with these texts and will feel confident enough to pursue further, independent study.

Because a number of different translation and transliteration styles are represented in this anthology, readers will notice that place and proper names may be spelled differently. For example, some will follow the Hebrew and refer to the matriarch Rivka, while others use the English equivalents, Rebecca or Rebekah.

Biblical quotes incorporated in rabbinic midrashim are printed in capital letters. Editorial insertions by translators or authors are bracketed ([ ]). My insertions are framed with these symbols: { }.

The rabbis tell us that there is no "earlier" or "later" in the Torah. By this they mean that the appearance of things in the text does not correlate to a chronological order for the purposes of interpretation. However, I think it can also be understood to mean that it is not too late to recover women's voices. We can do what our foremothers could not. We can study and interpret, and we can preserve our interpretation for ourselves and for our children's children.

An Introduction to Bible

The word *Torah* means "teaching," "path," or "way," but in the Jewish tradition, it has many more layers of meaning. In the widest sense, it refers to the totality of revelation. It can be understood to refer to the whole Bible, although it most commonly refers to the Five Books of Moses. We call the scroll on which these books are written—on parchment, by hand, and from which we read in the synagogue—Torah. The totality of our text tradition, including the Bible, Mishnah, Tosefta, the Babylonian and Jerusalem Talmuds, Midrash, and commentaries, can also be called Torah, as can the study of these texts. Torah is also the Jewish way of living, a way of life enriched and informed by these texts.

All of these meanings not only coexist, they occur at the same time: when we study the Book, we are standing at Sinai and receiving revelation—we are living Torah—and as we bring our own understanding and interpretations to the text, we are contributors to the totality of the tradition.

At the center is the Bible. It has many names. The most common name for the Jewish Bible in the West is the Old Testament. This is a Christian term, which is used to distinguish between the Jewish Bible and the New Testament. Some consider the term to be derogatory. Many people prefer to use the name TaNaKH, a word made up from the first letters of the Hebrew names of the three sections that make up the Bible. Those three sections are the Torah, or Teaching; Nevi'im, or Prophets; and Ketuvim, or Writings.

The first section of the TaNaKH, the Torah, includes the Five Books of Moses. Most English translations of the Bible label these books Genesis, Exodus, Leviticus, Numbers, and Deuteronomy. These names are taken from the ancient Greek translation of the Bible and they describe (if you understand Greek!) the contents or major theme of each book. The Hebrew names come from the opening word or words of the

xxi

book. In Hebrew, the book most of us know as Genesis is called Bereshit, or "In the beginning." Shemot is the Hebrew name for Exodus. It means "Names," and comes from the first verse, "These are the names of the sons of Israel who came to Egypt with Jacob . . ." Leviticus is called Vayikra in Hebrew, meaning "called," from the verse, "The Lord called to Moses and spoke to him from the Tent of Meeting, saying: . . ." Numbers is known as Bemidbar, "In the wilderness," from the verse "The Lord spoke to Moses in the Wilderness of Sinai . . . saying: . . ."[1] Devarim means "Words" and is the Hebrew name for Deuteronomy, from the verse, "These are the words that Moses addressed to all Israel on the other side of the Jordan . . ."

Sometimes the Torah is called the Pentateuch (Greek) or Humash (Hebrew), both of which are derived from the word for "five." The Torah is traditionally divided into fifty-four weekly synagogue readings, each known as a *parashah* (plural, *parshiyyot*). Each of these is usually read together with a specific selection from the Prophets, known as the *haftarah*.

The second section of the TaNaKH, called Nevi'im, or Prophets, is made up of Joshua, Judges, 1 Samuel, 2 Samuel, 1 Kings, 2 Kings, Isaiah, Jeremiah, Ezekiel, Hosea, Joel, Amos, Obadiah, Jonah, Micah, Nahum, Habakkuk, Zephaniah, Haggai, Zechariah, and Malachi. The first nine are predominately narrative, historical works. The last twelve, known as the Minor Prophets, are more literary or poetic.

The last section, known as Ketuvim, or Writings, includes Psalms, Proverbs, Job, The Song of Songs, Ruth, Lamentations, Ecclesiastes, Esther, Daniel, Ezra, Nehemiah, 1 Chronicles, and 2 Chronicles. This section includes a variety of literary forms, including poetry, historical accounts, wisdom literature, narratives, and prophecy.

The Bible has been translated more often than almost any other work, largely for Christian purposes. All of the translations differ. This is due in part to the fact that translators can work with different source documents. Catholic translations usually start with the Latin translation, and Protestant translations, with an English version. Because neither of

---

1. This translation follows the Artscroll Chumash. Nosson, Scherman, *The Chumash* (Brooklyn, NY: Mesorah Publications, 1993), p. 727.

these languages is the original, it is as if the translators were making a copy of a copy.

Jewish translations all start with the Hebrew text. Even so, there are differences between translations. Consider the following translations of the first sentence of the first book of the Bible, Genesis 1:1, all of which are from modern, Jewish publications:

> In the beginning God created the heaven and the earth (*The Holy Scriptures* [Tel Aviv: Sinai Publishing, 1979])

> When God began to create heaven and earth (*TaNaKH* [Philadelphia: Jewish Publication Society, 1985])

> In the beginning of God's creating the heavens and the earth (*The Chumash* [Brooklyn, NY: Mesorah Publications, 1993])

Translation is an inexact science, and well-qualified translators working from the identical source can still come up with different ways of expressing the Hebrew. Another factor has to do with the biases of the people doing the translating. Some people argue that translation is really interpretation, since in the end, translators must judge which English word or phrase best conveys the meaning of the Hebrew. This will be influenced by people's beliefs, and so a traditional translation will follow traditional commentaries while a translation incorporating the ideas of biblical criticism or the evidence of archaeology may follow those lines.

This points us to another important consideration. The Bible has been, and continues to be, studied through many lenses. From a traditional perspective, the Bible is the literal word of God delivered through the prophets. Tradition seems less concerned with inconsistencies than are many liberal Jews, who see them as opportunities for creative interpretation. The basic assumption of Midrash and the early commentators is that the text was a single, integrated work; every detail was important, and none was superfluous. The ancient idea that there is no "earlier" or "later" in the Torah makes it possible to compare anything and to interpret out of context.

Following from this, traditional study takes the text with all of its quirks as the starting point and attempts to discover the meaning inherent in unusual words, apparent contradictions, repetitions, and relationships, as well as the plain meaning.

Critical scholarship is a development of the modern period. It starts with the assumption that the Bible was written by human beings, incorporating a variety of older, oral traditions, which were compiled and edited at different times. This method looks to the elements of the text to determine which threads can be attributed to which tradition and to ascertain the agenda or perspective of the group or subgroup preserving the tradition. This approach is also informed by archaeology, modern historical analysis, and the study of non-Jewish texts and other ancient texts that are not included in the Bible. This approach can help to demonstrate the essential historicity of some elements of the Bible, and it also helps to concretize our "picture" of the world of our ancestors.

Literary criticism is more closely related to traditional text study, and may, in fact, have derived from it. Close reading of the text uncovers new meanings and, in doing so, reveals much about both the author and the reader.

Feminist criticism looks at the Bible with more than academic concern. The Bible has been used as a template for defining the roles of women. As such, it affects issues such as whether leadership roles are appropriate for women in the institutions of Judaism (and Christianity) and the relationships between men and women in family life. Feminist criticism looks at the way in which biblical models influence our present circumstances, but it also seeks to show that the Bible records only the perspectives of its human, male authors, however divinely inspired.

We should remember, when viewing the TaNaKH through these lenses, that we are looking at the ancient past through twentieth-century eyes. Our values are different than those of the biblical period, and it is possible that the women of that period did not feel oppressed by their circumstances. While the TaNaKH is not an egalitarian document, it does portray a wider variety of roles for women than the later Jewish tradition allowed.

This book will rely primarily on traditional interpretive techniques, especially where they intersect with literary criticism and feminist interpretation. As we will see, the idea that agendas or biases accompany the interpreter into the interpretation is not foreign to traditional interpretation.

All of this presupposes that Torah is worth studying, a question that many have answered negatively. Many of us own a Bible whose spine has never been cracked. Perhaps we are afraid of the sacredness of it or that we will not understand it—that it will be as inaccessible to our modern ears as Chaucer. Perhaps we took a peek once, maybe into Leviticus, and decided that detailed descriptions of sacrifices were not for us. Perhaps the message that Torah study is forbidden to women is too ingrained. Perhaps we are nervous that if we start reading the Bible, we will be subject to ridicule. Maybe we have been convinced that the Bible is a sexist document and not worth our time.

Nonetheless, you have picked up this book. Something is making you question those assumptions, letting you look at the TaNaKH with fresh eyes. The Bible has been around a long time; you might say to yourself, "There must be something to it." Or maybe your rebellious streak insisted that you take on what had been forbidden to you. Other people have found answers to difficult questions in the Bible, you think; perhaps you can, too. You may be the first woman in your family to have the opportunity to study. Perhaps you seek a sense of connection. Maybe you enjoy great literature. Whatever your reason, you have chosen to be part of the tradition of interpretation, interaction, puzzlement, and pleasure that has characterized Judaism's relationship with its sacred text.

Jill Hammer, whose midrash, "Leah's Blessing," appears in this volume, sets up two examples of women's responses to the demands of tradition in the characters of the biblical women Serach and Dinah. Dinah is portrayed as angry at the role that Judaism has insisted she accept and is searching for reasons to stay committed. She seems to speak for many of us who find that reading the TaNaKH is often an uneasy undertaking. The text is primarily the record of men's lives, and God is almost universally referred to in male language. Women do appear, but most often they are not independent actors, but supporting characters in the men's narratives. Layered over this is a long-standing tradition of exclusively male interpretation.

Serach, on the other hand, accepts what Judaism hands her, unquestioningly and naively. She is the symbol of those among us who have followed the path laid out for us willingly and acceptingly. In doing so, we blind ourselves to the inequities and rigid expectations that have limited us and that will limit our daughters.

Those of us who are angry and those of us who are accommodating each have an obligation to add our voices to the tradition of interpretation. We must do so to honor our foremothers—biblical and familial—who carried the essence of Judaism with them through the centuries, finding the strength to create and preserve a women's approach to Torah that they knew would be marginalized and almost lost. We must do so for our daughters, so that they will be strengthened and honored for their contributions, both within and outside traditional roles. Moreover, we must do so to "depatriarchalize" the tradition, so that it will be enriched with women's voices.

AN INTRODUCTION TO MIDRASH

The word *midrash* derives from the Hebrew root *daled-resh-shin*, which means "to seek," "to examine," and "to investigate." *Midrash* can be a confusing term because it is used to mean three different things. When someone refers to the Midrash ("the Midrash says"), they are usually referring to a series of compilations of interpretations of biblical verses. It can also be used to refer to a specific interpretation as in, "I know a midrash about Eve." Finally, the word can be used to refer to a particular method of interpretation. For the most part, when I use the word in this book, I will be referring to a specific example.

During the period of late antiquity, a group of men who derived their authority from their knowledge of Torah gained ascendancy in Judaism and created the core interpretive texts of Judaism. These men, who are known as the Sages or the Rabbis, believed that they were links in an unbroken chain of authority that began with the revelation of the Torah to Moses by God on Mount Sinai. The basis of that authority was a unique understanding of that revelation as transmitted via both oral and written traditions. Any man who mastered the material was admitted into their academy, and all who had been admitted were free to interpret and to teach. Although it was an entirely male institution, the rabbinate was elitist only in terms of intellect. Rabbis came from all social classes, and independently wealthy men sat side by side with charcoal makers. The rabbinate was not a profession as we often understand it today, and the Rabbis supported themselves and their families in the same ways that other Jews did.

The rabbinate became especially influential after the destruction of the Second Temple, when the priesthood, which had vied with the Rabbis for leadership of the Jewish people, lost its raison d' être. From the ashes of the Temple, the Rabbis created a revitalized Judaism that was no longer dependent on the Temple and the sacrificial cult. This was an amazing accomplishment in light of the theological crisis that the Temple's destruction had created. Judaism as we have known it is, in large part, the Judaism created by the Rabbis.

Midrash must be understood in the context of the two approaches that interweave within classic Jewish texts: halachah and aggadah. Halachah is a general way of referring to specifically legal material. Aggadah refers to the wide array of other rabbinic literature of the period, including narratives, parables, ethics, and homilies. Aggadah and halachah are not separate bodies of work, but are instead two different approaches. For example, an aggadic approach to the destruction of the Second Temple might attempt to console, while a halachic approach would consider the implications for the sacrificial cult. Midrash refers to a particular kind of interpretation, and midrashim can be either halachic or aggadic. Most of the time, when we speak of midrash, we mean midrash aggadah, and that is the type of midrash with which we will be concerned here.

Midrash was originally an oral tradition of commentary on specific books of the Bible. The various strands within it were collected and written down between 400 and 1200 C.E. These dates tell us only when the written record was created. Some of the material in them is much older.

Although the Midrashim were written over more than eight centuries, the Rabbis who wrote them shared a certain perspective. Gary G. Porton suggests five basic assumptions.[1] First, they assumed that every part of the Bible was written in a very precise way in order to teach something. Because of this, every nuance, from grammatical variations to repetitions and to the relative position of verses was, in a sense, a clue to deeper understanding. Related to this is the assumption that everything in the Bible—the Torah, the Prophets, and the Writings—was interrelated. With this understanding, the Rabbis could, for example, use a verse from one book to prove a point they were making about a passage in another book even though the two might have no apparent relationship.

The Rabbis also assumed that it was possible to have multiple

---

1. Gary G. Porton, *Understanding Rabbinic Midrash* (Hoboken, NJ: Ktav Publishing House, 1985), pp. 9–11.

interpretations of a single verse. As we will see, it is not unusual to have a variety of interpretations of a single event or person. The fourth assumption is that reason alone is not enough. Correct interpretations were arrived at only by combining faith and reason. As a result, one Rabbi might rebut another's conclusion by citing a biblical verse that appears to contradict it.

The fifth idea is perhaps the most important one. The Rabbis believed that making midrash was a sacred activity. Midrash was the way in which they expressed their relationship with God, with all the complexity of emotion that any lifelong relationship entails. Study and interpretation, in their view, led to redemption of the world by bringing God's presence into it.

Midrash is not only a means of extracting meaning from the Bible. It is also a way of reading meaning *into* the text. Jacob Neusner, one of the most important scholars in the field, explains that when the Rabbis sought to compose midrashim, they relied on the Bible, not strictly as a source to be interpreted, but "to serve a purpose defined not by Scripture but by a faith under construction and subject to articulation. Scripture formed a dictionary, providing a vast range of permissible usages of intelligible words."[2] He suggests that for the Rabbis, the Bible was like the palette of colors that an artist uses to create a painting; the paint is not the painting. In other words, the Rabbis wrote with an agenda in mind. They sought to reconstruct or renew Judaism to reflect the new reality in which they found themselves. In order to speak in an authentic, authoritative manner, they used the language of the Bible—the stories, metaphors, promises, and prophecies—to construct the new system.

Other scholars think that midrash had a different purpose. Where Neusner starts with the assumption that the Bible served as the paint from which the Rabbis created paintings in the form of midrashim, others see the Bible as the painting itself, and as subject to a variety of interpretations. As Neusner sees it, the rabbinic agenda was to legitimize the new theology. Others see the agenda as demonstrating the continuing relevance of the Bible, an issue as troublesome to the Rabbis as it is to us today.

---

2. Jacob Neusner, *The Midrash: An Introduction* (Northvale, NJ: Jason Aronson, 1990), p. xi.

To meet the challenge of continuing relevance, Judah Goldin argues, "Judaism adopts not the neutral and descriptive terms of change and adaption, but a view of revelation which is permanently at work through an activity called 'Midrash.'"[3] With midrash, attention is given, not only to the current circumstances, but also to the tradition that has helped to define the community in all its particulars. In this way, change does not threaten a complete break with the past, and is in fact seen as part of Gods original revelation.

In both views, Midrash is a way of integrating change and tradition. In one view, the agenda comes first, and the tradition is the tool by which it is implemented. From the other perspective, the appropriate response to change is contained within the tradition, and the midrashic method is the means by which the Sages discover it. Midrash was the rabbinic technique for coping with profound theological and social changes, a technique that permitted radical transformation without severing ties to the past.

There is much debate as to whether modern interpretations of biblical verses, narratives, or individuals should rightly be called midrash. Contemporary interpretations can be found in a number of different formats, from novels that expand on biblical themes to one- or two-line insights into a single verse or personality. While all share a common "midrashic impulse"[4] to take the Bible as a starting point, these interpretations differ in methodology and intent. These factors, as well as age and sanctity, distinguish the newer material from the ancient body of work, and some suggest that the distinction should be preserved by limiting the use of the term "midrash" to the rabbinic sources.

A second issue is the question of who are the legitimate inheritors of the midrashic tradition. From a traditional perspective, the answer is rabbis, and great ones at that. Among liberal Jews, the answer is not so clear. Perhaps anyone can make midrash, and time will determine what is preserved and

---

3. Judah Goldin, "Of Change and Adaptation in Judaism," in *Studies in Midrash and Related Literature*, ed. Barry L. Eichler and Jeffrey H. Tigay (Philadelphia: Jewish Publication Society, 1988), p. 221.

4. David C. Jacobson, *Modern Midrash* (Albany, NY: State University of New York Press, 1987), p. 3.

what is left behind. Moreover, how do we determine what constitutes contemporary midrash as distinguished from fairy tales or fiction?

On the other hand, there are compelling reasons to call some of the contemporary material midrash. Not all of the works that draw on biblical images have enough in common with the midrashic process to rightly be considered a part of that tradition, but many do. The important issue is not so much the time in which the interpretation is written, but the method that is used and the intent of the author. Writers who use the Bible's own language to reinterpret it and who share at least in part the five underlying rabbinic assumptions have some claim to a midrashic methodology. When those same authors write with religious intent—to explore theological issues or even to draw closer to God—the claim is even stronger.

There are other ideological reasons for laying claim to the term "midrash." Scholars agree that midrash was the rabbinic method of coping with social, political, and theological change and of integrating that change into tradition. We find ourselves today in a period as traumatic and uncertain as the rabbinic period. We are still grappling with the myriad effects of the Shoah (Holocaust) and the establishment of the State of Israel. We are still trying to figure out how to remain a people when we are all, to some extent, Jews by choice. We are also grappling with issues of the wider culture—such as feminism. Midrash was the way in which Judaism dealt with such things in the past, and it succeeded because it accommodated change without breaking with tradition. By naming our work midrash, we assert our tie to the past and insist that we, like our ancestors, can accommodate change without succumbing to it.

Although contemporary interpretations do not have the same sense of sanctity or authority, it is important to link them to tradition and thus declare that what we are doing now is linked to what was done then. By claiming the title, we assert that we are a legitimate part of the ongoing process of interpretation. To do less is to define ourselves out of the chain of tradition. This is an especially important point for women, who for so long were excluded from the process.

All of the contemporary works selected for this volume were written using a midrashic mindset. They use the language of the Bible to explore and integrate change and to uncover the women's Torah—the Torah of the white spaces. Consider the following:

> One way for women to relieve the tension created in a relationship between the static written Torah and the modern changing world is for each generation to read the text with fresh and open eyes. Women's roles in the Torah were circumscribed and limited while women's roles in the modern world are expanding. Therefore, it is incumbent upon contemporary women to study the text and to write modern stories that maintain a relationship with the text, incorporating their own experiences and consciousness into Judaism. This midrashic process allows Judaism to grow and develop a healthy relationship with all of its people.[5]

I don't want to rewrite the Bible; I want to make it ours by having it reflect women's reality as well as men's. In other words, our task in writing interpretative works, or midrash, is to put woman's voice back where it should have been in the first place. This kind of midrash does not detract from or undermine the Torah, rather it adds additional dimensions to the Torah by making it contemporaneous, relevant and religiously meaningful.[6]

These retellings confront each of these themes in a spirit of tikkun olam (the repairing or healing of the world). Tikkun olam is the essence of the holy covenant: that redemption of the world will be effected only through a joint effort of God and humanity. Part of that effort, in my view, is the creation of an inclusive religious language that affirms all people. Because of its power to shape and create meaning and value, we need a language of God, humanity, and God's covenant that cherishes each person's unique (not role-bound) gifts. After 3 millennia of excluding women, tikkun olam demands nothing less than the presence of a specifically feminine language to exist alongside the all-too-familiar traditional masculine language.[7]

---

5. Jane Sprague Zones, "Introduction: Begetting a Midrash," in *Taking the Fruit: Modern Women's Tales of the Bible*, ed. Jane Sprague Zones (San Diego, CA: Women's Institute for Continuing Jewish Education, 1989), p. 6.

6. Naomi Graetz, *S/He Created Them* (Chapel Hill, NC: Professional Press, 1993), p. 4.

7. Karen Prager, private correspondence to author. August 24, 1995.

For all of these reasons, women interpreters have a right to name their work midrash, although not all of the authors do.

It is important—for many reasons, among them clarity—to distinguish between the bodies of work. I will refer to the ancient interpretations as rabbinic or traditional midrashim. The modern material will be identified as contemporary or women's midrashim.

HOW TO STUDY

Reading Jewish texts requires an active engagement with the text. Barry W. Holtz explains it this way:

> The rabbis throughout Jewish history were essentially *readers*. The text was Torah; the task to read that text. We tend usually to think of reading as a passive occupation, but for the Jewish textual tradition, it was anything but that. Reading was a passionate and active grappling with God's living word. It held the challenge of uncovering secret meanings, unheard-of explanations, matters of great weight and significance. An active, indeed interactive, reading was their method of approaching the sacred text called Torah and through that reading process of finding something at once new and very old.[1]

In this way, he continues, "Reading thus becomes less an act of self-reflection than a way of communal identification and communication. One studies to become part of the Jewish people itself."[2]

In fact, traditional Jewish study occurs in a social context. Two individuals team up to study together on a regular basis. Typically, a lesson is laid out for the larger group, the students go to the *beit midrash*, or study hall, where they struggle together over the texts. The large group reconvenes, and the students discuss their findings. Partners learn, not only about the texts, but about themselves and each other. Consider the following ancient commentary: "'And acquire yourself a friend.' How so? This teaches that a person should acquire a friend to eat with, drink with, read Torah with, study Mishnah with, sleep with, and to whom all secrets

---

1. Barry W. Holtz, "Introduction: On Reading Jewish Texts," in *Back to the Sources*, ed. Barry W. Holtz (New York: Summit Books, 1984), p. 16.
2. Ibid., p. 18.

will be told—secrets of Torah and secrets of everyday affairs."[3] Contemporary scholarship on adult learning reinforces this model. In it, lines are blurred between teacher and student, and students are empowered to take responsibility for their own learning.

Consequently, it should not be surprising that I suggest that you "acquire yourself a friend" as you begin your studies. Try to find someone who has a similar level of knowledge so that you can avoid the roles of teacher and pupil. Your partner can be male or female, although most women with whom I have worked prefer to work with another woman, especially at the beginning. The two of you can study together, or you can be part of a larger group of pairs.

Set aside a regular time to meet. Try for once a week if you can, or else maybe once a month. If you meet less frequently, you will lose some of the dynamics that this kind of study generates. Set up a lesson for yourselves. You can use a section of a chapter or an entire chapter, depending on the time you have set aside. One to two hours is a good length to start. For your first meeting, for example, the two of you might decide that you will focus on the biblical passages concerning Eve and Lilith. Work at a table if you can, sitting across from one another. It is helpful if you each have a copy of the text, but not necessary. One of you might read the section out loud to the other, or perhaps you can take turns reading and listening. Then, go over the text once again, stopping to discuss the details you have noticed or questions you may have. (Each of the chapters in the second part of the book have some questions to help guide you.) There are no right or wrong answers.

If you are studying with a group of people, have the whole group meet first for a few minutes. Wrap up any outstanding questions from the last session, and set your goals for the current session. Perhaps last time you studied the biblical selections on Rebecca. You may want to refresh your memories on the key points that you discovered, especially if it has been a while since your last meeting. Then break into pairs, always with your regular partner. Try to find a corner where the two of you can concentrate on one another's comments, but keep in mind that the background noise is characteristic of this kind of study (remember the yeshiva scene in the

3. *Avot de Rabbi Nathan*, Ch. 8, author's translation.

movie *Yentl?*). After a specified period of time (thirty minutes to one hour), reconvene as a large group. Take turns talking about the interesting details, connections, ideas, and so forth that you have uncovered. It is usually interesting to see the different directions that each group takes.

While you will certainly gain more from this type of active study, please do not be discouraged from just sitting down and reading the book by yourself. All Torah study is good, and there is much to be said for silent contemplation, also.

No matter how you are studying, always begin with the biblical excerpts. They are the foundation for all of the interpretation, both rabbinic and contemporary, and the later material will make much more sense to you if you understand the source on which they draw.

Studying the Bible is a fascinating process, for no matter how many times you read a passage, you will find that there is even more to be uncovered. It is, as Joel Rosenberg says, "a mischievous companion":[4]

> For while biblical narrative unfolds in a plain and ingenious voice, its sticky surface soon becomes apparent. Details are omitted that we must fill in with the imagination—or perhaps leave unfilled. Characters' thoughts are concealed, and their actions and words admit of several interpretations. Options seem closed off by choices the characters make, but consequences of the choices are often delayed for several story cycles. Turns of phrase become significant and wordplay seems to multiply. The forward movement of fictional time yields, on closer reading, to a more subtle interplay of flashback, repetition, quotation, allusion, dream-visioning and waking, prospective and retrospective glance, fade-out and fade-in—all of which make time seem to proceed in a mottled and disjunctive fashion. Non sequiturs and digressions complicate the screen of discourse, and stories sometimes suspend their actions at particularly tense and weighted moments, only to pick them up at a later stage, creating a text riddled with gaps, discontinuities, and irresolution. Characters come to the fore out of nowhere, and disappear just as abruptly. Even key characters are kept in view only as long as they are useful to the plot.
>
> Above all, motifs return; all action seems haunted by predecessors. A

---

4. Joel Rosenberg, "Bible: Biblical Narrative," in *Back to the Sources*, ed. Barry W. Holtz (New York: Summit Books, 1984), p. 31.

universe of echoes and resemblances emerges, and characters and eras seem to struggle to free themselves from the grip of sameness and from the fugal counterpoint woven by repetition. And when resolutions come, as in places they must, they do not let the text yield its prerogatives of mystery making and complication. To read biblical narrative is to submit oneself to a lesson in *how* to read.[5]

Read the text once or twice to familiarize yourself with the characters, situation, and plot. (If you have access to a Judaica library, it can be helpful to study there. Then you can use tools like the *Encyclopaedia Judaica*, an analytical concordance (a reference volume that lists all the places where a word, name, or place appears in the Bible and gives some explanation), or Bible dictionary to clarify the "who, what, where, when, and why." Then, read the text a third time, looking for motifs, key words, themes, tense changes, unusual words, names (or lack thereof), or other intriguing details. Think about your discoveries. What is missing—and why? Why is a particular detail included? If you can, refer back to the original Hebrew on words or phrases that trouble you, or check another translation.

Next, turn to the rabbinic midrashim. Reading midrash is also challenging. For one thing, even in English the syntax is difficult to follow, and often, midrashim are based upon a Hebrew word-play or pun of a biblical word. The Rabbis use a shorthand method of identifying biblical verses by citing a few words on the assumption that the reader will know, not only the full verse, but its context as well. It takes a while to get used to the rhythms and images. In some respects, it is like reading Shakespeare or Chaucer.

If you own a TaNaKH or have access to one, you may want to have it handy. As you read the midrashim in this collection, determine the biblical verse or passage that is being interpreted or cited as a prooftext (a verse quoted by the rabbis to prove the point they are making) and look it up. Read, not only the particular verse, but enough to determine the context. What came before, and what follows? Where are you in the narrative? Think for a moment about the passage. Is there anything troubling about it? Think not only about the content, but about the

---

5. Ibid., p. 32.

grammar and other details. Ask yourself why the passage was written in this particular way.

After you have become fairly comfortable with the biblical text with which you are dealing, read the traditional midrash. You may have to read it a couple of times until you are clear about what it is saying. Sometimes, it helps to read it out loud. If you have a study partner, take turns reading it to each other.

Once you are clear on what the Rabbis are saying, see if you can determine the problem they are trying to solve or what is troubling them. Your earlier close reading of the biblical text will help you here. If you have a partner, discuss the interpretation. What is behind their interpretation? What agenda might the Rabbis have had? How well do you think they addressed the problem? Do you think they were addressing the right issue? What is the relevance of their answer to today's world and to you?

Next, turn to the contemporary midrash. Because they have been written in modern English, you will find them easier to read, but do not let this stop you from reading closely and actively. Follow the same procedure you did for the rabbinic midrash, and ask the same questions.

Now, compare the two midrashim. In what ways were the interpretations similar—and different? How do you think the time, place, gender, and other characteristics of the interpreters affected their answers? Were they addressing the same issue? If so, what is it about the issue that drew to the same place people separated by great gulfs of time and culture? If the rabbinic and contemporary commentators spoke to different aspects of the biblical passage, speculate on the reasons why. How do the contemporary interpreters integrate ideas from the rabbinic midrashim?

In other words, engage the texts. Flirt with them. Argue with them. Close the book and stomp away if they make you angry, but come back to them. They are yours.

We All Stood Together
for Rachel Adler
by Merle Feld

My brother and I were at Sinai
He kept a journal
of what he saw
of what he heard
of what it all meant to him

I wish I had such a record
of what happened to me there

It seems like every time I want to write
I can't
I'm always holding a baby
one of my own
or one for a friend
always holding a baby
so my hands are never free
to write things down

And then
as time passes
the particulars
the hard data
the who what when where why
slip away from me

and all I'm left with is
the feeling

But feelings are just sounds
the vowel barking of a mute

My brother is so sure of what he heard
after all he's got a record of it
consonant after consonant after consonant

If we remembered it together
we could recreate holy time
sparks flying

1

LILITH AND EVE

Lilith and Eve in the Bible

As you will see, the TaNaKH presents two versions of the creation of Woman.
From this, some have concluded that two different women were created, one
with Adam and one from him. The First Woman seems to disappear from the
narrative as Eve takes center stage.

Eve, and the First Woman, whom some call Lilith, are seen differently
than any other of the women that share the pages of the Bible with them. They
are the archetypes for all women. Commentators rarely see them as individuals,
but rather as the essence of what women are or are supposed to be.

Contemporary scholars see the roots of these stories in the wider culture in
which the early Israelites lived, but we have made them our own. Let us take
a look at what the Bible has to say about them. Note that Lilith is only alluded
to and not directly mentioned in the creation narratives, and that her role as
First Woman is absent from the passage from Isaiah.

As you read, compare the two accounts of the creation of woman. What
are the key elements that distinguish the two narratives? Compare the way in
which God communicates with these new beings in each account. Look
especially carefully at God's instructions to Adam concerning the tree of
knowledge, the serpent's question to Eve, and her response.

The name Lilith only appears once in the TaNaKH, in the passage cited *below. Some translations interpret the Hebrew to mean screech owl; others, including this translation, see it as the name of a female demon. What does this passage tell us about the nature of Lilith?*

And God said, "Let us make man in our image, after our likeness. They shall rule the fish of the sea, the birds of the sky, the cattle, the whole earth, and all the creeping things that creep on the earth." And God created man in His image, in the image of God He created him; male and female He created them. God blessed them and God said to them, "Be fertile and increase, fill the earth and master it; and rule the fish of the sea, the birds of the sky, and all the living things that creep on earth" (Genesis 1:26–28).

. . . When the Lord God made earth and heaven—when no shrub of the field was yet on earth and no grasses of the field had yet sprouted, because the Lord God had not sent rain upon the earth and there was no man to till the soil, but a flow would well up from the ground and water the whole surface of the earth—the Lord God formed man from the dust of the earth. He blew into his nostrils the breath of life, and man became a living being (Genesis 2:4–9).

. . . The Lord God took the man and placed him in the garden of Eden, to till it and tend it. And the Lord God commanded the man, saying, "Of every tree of the garden you are free to eat; but as for the tree of knowledge of good and bad, you must not eat of it; for as soon as you eat of it, you shall die."

The Lord God said, "It is not good for man to be alone; I will make a fitting helper for him." And the Lord God formed out of the earth all the wild beasts and all the birds of the sky, and brought them to the man to see what he would call them; and whatever the man called each living creature, that would be its name. And the man gave names to all the cattle and to the birds of the sky and to all the wild beasts; but for Adam no fitting helper was found. So the Lord God cast a deep sleep upon the man; and, while he slept, He took one of his ribs and closed up the flesh at that spot. And the Lord God fashioned the rib that He had taken from the man into a woman; and He brought her to the man. Then the man said,

> "This one at last
> Is bone of my bones
> And flesh of my flesh.
> This one shall be called Woman,
> For from man was she taken."

Hence a man leaves his father and mother and clings to his wife, so that they become one flesh.

The two of them were naked, the man and his wife, yet they felt no shame. Now the serpent was the shrewdest of all the wild beasts that the Lord God had made. He said to the woman, "Did God really say: 'You shall not eat of any tree of the garden?'" The woman replied to the serpent, "We may eat of the fruit of the other trees of the garden. It is only about the fruit of the tree in the middle of the garden that God said: 'You shall not eat of it or touch it, lest you die.'" And the serpent said to the woman, "You are not going to die, but God knows that as soon as you eat of it your eyes will be opened and you will be like divine beings who know good and bad." When the woman saw that the tree was good for eating and a delight to the eyes, and that the tree was desirable as a source of wisdom, she took of its fruit and ate. She also gave some to her husband, and he ate. Then the eyes of both of them were opened and they perceived that they were naked; and they sewed together fig leaves and made themselves loincloths.

They heard the sound of the Lord God moving about in the garden at the breezy time of day; and the man and his wife hid from the Lord God among the trees of the garden. The Lord God called out to the man and said to him, "Where are you?" He replied, "I heard the sound of You in the garden, and I was afraid because I was naked, so I hid." Then He asked, "Who told you that you were naked? Did you eat of the tree from which I had forbidden you to eat?" The man said, "The woman You put at my side—she gave me of the tree, and I ate." And the Lord God said to the woman, "What is this you have done!" The woman replied, "The serpent duped me, and I ate." Then the Lord God said to the serpent,

> "Because you did this,
> More cursed shall you be
> Than all cattle

And all the wild beasts:
On your belly shall you crawl
And dirt shall you eat
All the days of your life.
I will put enmity
Between you and the woman,
And between your offspring and hers;
They shall strike at your head,
And you shall strike at their heel."

And to the woman He said,

"I will make most severe
Your pangs in childbearing;
In pain shall you bear children,
Yet your urge shall be for your husband,
And he shall rule over you."

To Adam He said, "Because you did as your wife said and ate of the tree about which I commanded you, 'You shall not eat of it,'

"Cursed be the ground because of you;
By toil shall you eat of it
All the days of your life:
Thorns and thistles shall it sprout for you.
But your food shall be the grasses of the field;
By the sweat of your brow
Shall you get bread to eat,
Until you return to the ground—
For from it you were taken.
For dust you are,
And to dust you shall return."

The man named his wife Eve, because she was the mother of all the living. And the Lord God made garments of skins for Adam and his wife, and clothed them.

And the Lord God said, "Now that the man has become like one of us, knowing good and bad, what if he should stretch out his hand and take also from the tree of life and eat, and live forever!" So the Lord God banished him from the garden of Eden, to till the soil from which he was taken. He drove the man out, and stationed east of the garden of Eden the cherubim and the fiery ever-turning sword, to guard the way to the tree of life (Genesis 2:15–3:24)

> For it is the Lord's day of retribution,
> The year of vindication for Zion's cause.
> Its streams shall be turned to pitch
> And its soil to sulfur.
> Its land shall become burning pitch,
> Night and day it shall never go out;
> Its smoke shall rise for all time.
> Through the ages it shall lie in ruins;
> Through the aeons none shall traverse it.
> Jackdaws and owls shall possess it;
> Great owls and ravens shall dwell there.
> He shall measure it with a line of chaos
> And with weights of emptiness.
> It shall be called, "No kingdom is there,"
> Its nobles and all its lords shall be nothing.
> Thorns shall grow up in its palaces,
> Nettles and briers in its strongholds.
> It shall be a home of jackals,
> An abode of ostriches.
> Wildcats shall meet hyenas,
> Goat-demons shall greet each other;
> There too the lilith shall repose
> And find herself a resting place. (Isaiah 34:8–14)

Rabbinic Midrashim

As you read these midrashim about Eve and Lilith, compare the qualities and roles that are assigned to each of them. In what ways are these interpretations tied to the biblical text, and where do they depart from it? Why are these particular questions asked and these answers given? Would you ask the same questions—or give the same answers? How do you think these interpretations may have influenced the way in which Judaism views women?

The last midrash is from a collection dating from the Middle Ages, making it far less ancient than the rest of the midrashic material included in this anthology. "The Alphabet of Ben Sirah" was, according to contemporary scholars, written as a satirical work, although it is generally accepted as part of the midrashic tradition. Many of its more heretical elements were probably censored by the scribes, which may have contributed to its acceptance. Because of the prominence of Lilith in contemporary interpretations of the origins of human beings, I have chosen to include it.

R. Joshua of Siknin said in R. Levi's name: . . . He considered well . . . from what part to create her. Said He: "I will not create her from {Adam's} head, lest she be swellheaded; nor from the eye, lest she be a coquette; nor from the ear, lest she be an eavesdropper; nor from the mouth, lest she be a gossip; nor from the heart, lest she be prone to jealousy; nor from the hand, lest she be light-fingered; nor from the foot, lest she be a gadabout; but from the modest part of man, for even when he stands naked, that part is covered." And as He created each limb He ordered her, "Be a modest woman." Yet in spite of all of this, BUT YE HAVE SET AT NOUGHT ALL MY COUNSEL, AND WOULD NONE OF MY REPROOF (Proverbs 1:25). "I did not create her from the head, yet she is swellheaded, as it is written, THEY WALK WITH STRETCHED-FORTH NECKS (Isaiah 3:16); nor from the eye, yet she is a coquette: AND WANTON EYES (ibid.); nor from the ear, yet she is an eavesdropper: NOW SARAH LISTENED IN THE TENT DOOR (Genesis 18:10); nor from the heart, yet she is prone to jealousy: RACHEL ENVIED HER SISTER (ibid., 30:1); nor from the hand, yet she is light-fingered: AND RACHEL STOLE THE TERAPHIM (ibid., 31:19); nor from the foot, yet she is a gadabout: AND DINAH WENT OUT, etc. (ibid., 34:1)."[1]

---

1. *Genesis Rabbah* 18:2, in *The Midrash*, ed. and trans. H. Freedman and Maurice Simon et al. (London: Soncino Press, 1951).

A Caesar once said to Rabban Gamliel: "Your God is a thief, for it is written, AND THE LORD GOD CAUSED A DEEP SLEEP TO FALL UPON ADAM, AND HE TOOK ONE OF HIS RIBS" (Genesis 2:21). Rabban Gamliel's daughter said, "Leave him to me and I will answer him." [Turning to Caesar], she said, "Send me a police officer." "Why do you need one?" he asked. She replied, "Thieves came to us during the night and took a silver pitcher from us, leaving one of gold in its place." "Would that such a thief came to us every day," he exclaimed. "Ah!" said she, "was it not Adam's gain that he was deprived of a rib and given a wife to serve him?"[2]

R. Joshua was asked . . . why must a woman use perfume? "Man was created from earth," he answered, "and earth never putrefies, but Eve was created from a bone. For example: if you leave meat three days unsalted, it immediately goes putrid." "And why has a woman a penetrating [shrill] voice, but not a man?" "I will give you an illustration," replied he. "If you fill a pot with meat it does not make any sound, but when you put a bone into it, the sound [of sizzling] spreads immediately." "And why is man easily appeased, but not a woman?" "Man was created from the earth," he answered, "and when you pour a drop of water on it, it immediately absorbs it; but Eve was created from a bone, which even if you soak many days in water does not become saturated."[3]

Moses said to Him: THE INHABITANTS OF THE LAND . . . HAVE HEARD THAT THOU LORD ART IN THE MIDST OF THIS PEOPLE . . . NOW IF THOU SHALT KILL THIS PEOPLE AS ONE MAN (Numbers 14:14–15). . . . Another exposition: Do not do it, that the nations of the world may not regard you as a cruel Being and say: "The Generation of the Flood came and He destroyed them, the Generation of the Separation [those that built the Tower of Babel] came and He destroyed them, the Sodomites and the Egyptians came and He destroyed them, and these also, whom he called MY SON, MY

---

2. Babylonian Talmud, *Sanhedrin* 39a. *The Book of Legends*, ed. Hayim Nahman Bialik and Yehoshua Hana Ravnitzky; trans. William G. Braude (New York: Schocken Books, 1992).

3. *Genesis Rabbah* 17:8, in ibid.

FIRSTBORN (Exodus 4:22), He is now destroying! As that Lilith
(*kelilith*) who, when she finds nothing else turns upon her own children,
so BECAUSE THE LORD WAS NOT ABLE TO BRING THIS
PEOPLE INTO THE LAND . . . HE HATH SLAIN THEM" (Numbers 14:16).[4]

R. Ḥanina said: One may not sleep in a house alone, and whoever
sleeps in a house alone is seized by Lilith.[5]

Soon afterward the young son of the king took ill. Said Nebuchadnezzar, "Heal my son. If you don't I will kill you." Ben Sira immediately
sat down and wrote an amulet with the Holy Name, and he inscribed on
it the angels in charge of medicine by their names, forms, and images, and
by their wings, hands, and feet. Nebuchadnezzar looked at the amulet.
"Who are these?"
  "The angels who are in charge of medicine: Snvi {Sanvi}, Snsvi
{Sansanvi}, and Smnglof {Semangelaf}. After God created Adam, who
was alone, He said, 'It is not good for man to be alone' (Genesis 2:18).
He then created a woman for Adam, from the earth, as He had created
Adam himself, and called her Lilith. Adam and Lilith immediately began
to fight. She said, 'I will not lie below,' and he said, 'I will not lie beneath
you, but only on top. For you are fit only to be in the bottom position,
while I am to be in the superior one.' Lilith responded, 'We are equal to
each other inasmuch as we were both created from the earth.' But they
would not listen to one another. When Lilith saw this, she pronounced
the Ineffable Name and flew away into the air. Adam stood in prayer
before his Creator: 'Sovereign of the universe!' he said, 'the woman you
gave me has run away.' At once, the Holy One, blessed be He, sent these
three angels to bring her back.
  "Said the Holy One to Adam, 'If she agrees to come back, fine. If not,
she must permit one hundred of her children to die every day.' The angels
left God and pursued Lilith, whom they overtook in the midst of the sea,

---

4. *Numbers Rabbah* 16:25, in ibid.
5. Babylonian Talmud, *Shabbat* 151b, in *The Babylonian Talmud*, ed. and
trans. I. Epstein et al. (London: Soncino Press, 1935–1952).

in the mighty waters wherein the Egyptians were destined to drown. They told her God's word, but she did not wish to return. The angels said, 'We shall drown you in the sea.'

"'Leave me!' She said. 'I was created only to cause sickness to infants. If the infant is male, I have dominion over him for eight days after his birth, and if a female, for twenty days.'

"When the angels heard Lilith's words, they insisted she go back. But she swore to them by the name of the living and eternal God: 'Whenever I see you or your names or your forms in an amulet, I will have no power over that infant.' She also agreed to have one hundred of her demons perish, and for the same reason, we write the angels' names on the amulets of young children. When Lilith sees their names, she remembers her oath and the child recovers."[6]

Applesauce for Eve

by Marge Piercy

Marge Piercy's poem seems to me to be a midrash especially on Genesis 3:6, WHEN THE WOMAN SAW THAT THE TREE WAS GOOD FOR EATING AND DELIGHT TO THE EYES, AND THAT THE TREE WAS DESIRABLE AS A SOURCE OF WISDOM, SHE TOOK OF THE FRUIT AND ATE. How do you think the Rabbis understood that verse? How did you read it? What do you think of this interpretation?

> Those old daddies cursed you and us in you,
> damned for your curiosity: for your sin
> was wanting knowledge. To try, to taste,
> to take into the body, into the brain
> and turn each thing, each sign, each factoid

---

6. "The Alphabet of Ben Sira," in *Rabbinic Fantasies: Imaginative Narratives from Classical Hebrew Literature*, ed. David Stern and Mark Jay Mirsky; trans. Norman Bronznick et al. (Philadelphia: Jewish Publication Society, 1990), pp. 183–184.

round and round as new facets glint and white
fractures into colors and the image breaks
into crystal fragments that pierce the nerves
while the brain cast the chips into patterns.

Each experiment sticks a finger deep in the pie,
dares existence, blows a horn in the ear
of belief, lets the nasty and difficult brats
of real questions into the still air
of the desiccated parlor of stasis.
What we all know to be true, constant,
melts like frost landscapes on a window
in a jet of steam. How many last words
in how many dead languages would translate into,
But what happens if I, and Whoops!

We see Adam wagging his tail, good dog, good
dog, while you and the snake shimmy up the tree,
lab partners in a dance of will and hunger,
that thirst not of the flesh but of the brain.
Men always think women are wanting sex,
cock, snake, when it is the world she's after.
The birth trauma for the first conceived kid
of the ego, I think therefore I am, I
kick the tree, who am I, why am I,
going, going to die, die, die.

You are indeed the mother of invention,
the first scientist. Your name means
life: finite, dynamic, swimming against
the current of time, tasting, testing,
eating knowledge like any other nutrient.
We are all the children of your bright hunger.
We are all products of that first experiment,
for if death was the worm in that apple,
the seeds were freedom and the flowering of choice.

Our Story: The Coming of Lilith

by Judith Plaskow

Judith Plaskow's much-quoted story uses biblical figures to address contemporary issues. Do you think the Rabbis did the same thing in their interpretations? How did they do so? How might Jewish tradition have developed had this interpretation of the Garden of Eden tale been the predominant one?

In the beginning, the Lord God formed Adam and Lilith from the dust of the ground and breathed into their nostrils the breath of life. Created from the same source, both having been formed from the ground, they were equal in all ways. Adam, being a man, didn't like this situation, and he looked for ways to change it. He said, "I'll have my figs now, Lilith," ordering her to wait on him, and he tried to leave her the daily tasks of life in the garden. But Lilith wasn't one to take any nonsense; she picked herself up, uttered God's holy name, and flew away. "Well, now, Lord," complained Adam, "that uppity woman you sent me has gone and deserted me." The Lord, inclined to be sympathetic, sent his messengers after Lilith, telling her to shape up and return to Adam or face dire punishment. She, however, preferring anything to living with Adam, decided to stay where she was. And so God, after more careful consideration this time, caused a deep sleep to fall on Adam and out of one of his ribs created for him a second companion, Eve.

For a time, Eve and Adam had a good thing going. Adam was happy now, and Eve, though she occasionally sensed capacities within herself that remained undeveloped, was basically satisfied with the role of Adam's wife and helper. The only thing that really disturbed her was the excluding closeness of the relationship between Adam and God. Adam and God just seemed to have more in common, both being men, and Adam came to identify with God more and more. After a while, that made God a bit uncomfortable too, and he started going over in his mind whether he may not have made a mistake letting Adam talk him into banishing Lilith and creating Eve, seeing the power that gave Adam.

Meanwhile Lilith, all alone, attempted from time to time to rejoin the human community in the garden. After her first fruitless attempt to breach its walls, Adam worked hard to build them stronger, even getting Eve to help him. He told her fearsome stories of the demon Lilith who threatens women in childbirth and steals children from their cradles in the middle of the night. The second time Lilith came, she stormed the garden's main gate, and a great battle ensued between her and Adam in which she was finally defeated. This time, however, before Lilith got away, Eve got a glimpse of her and saw she was a woman like herself.

After this encounter, seeds of curiosity and doubt began to grow in Eve's mind. Was Lilith indeed just another woman? Adam had said she was a demon. Another woman! The very idea attracted Eve. She had never seen another creature like herself before. And how beautiful and strong Lilith looked! How bravely she had fought! Slowly, slowly, Eve began to think about the limits of her own life within the garden.

One day, after many months of strange and disturbing thoughts, Eve, wandering around the edge of the garden, noticed a young apple tree she and Adam had planted, and saw that one of its branches stretched over the garden wall. Spontaneously, she tried to climb it, and struggling to the top, swung herself over the wall.

She did not wander long on the other side before she met the one she had come to find, for Lilith was waiting. At first sight of her, Eve remembered the tales of Adam and was frightened, but Lilith understood and greeted her kindly. "Who are you?" they asked each other, "What is your story?" And they sat and spoke together, of the past and then of the future. They talked for many hours, not once, but many times. They taught each other many things, and told each other stories, and laughed together, and cried, over and over, till the bond of sisterhood grew between them.

Meanwhile, back in the garden, Adam was puzzled by Eve's comings and goings, and disturbed by what he sensed to be her new attitude toward him. He talked to God about it, and God, having his own problems with Adam and a somewhat broader perspective, was able to help out a little—but he was confused, too. Something had failed to go according to plan. As in the days of Abraham, he needed counsel from his children. "I am who I am," thought God, "but I must become who I will become."

And God and Adam were expectant and afraid the day Eve and Lilith returned to the garden, bursting with possibilities, ready to rebuild it together.

2

SARAH AND HAGAR

Sarah and Hagar in the Bible

Sarah, our first Matriarch, appears in the TaNaKH in Genesis 11:32 in a genealogical passage that carries humanity forward from the time of Noah and the Tower of Babel to that of Abraham, Sarah's husband and the first Patriarch. On God's command, the couple set out together to build a great nation in a new land. At that time, they were called Sarai and Abram. They were only to earn their new, God-given names after a lifetime together. We know nothing of Sarai's life before her marriage to Abram but, by biblical standards, we have a relatively full picture of her life as an adult.

As with Sarah, the biblical account tells us nothing about Hagar's life before she was swept up into the drama of nation-building other than that she was Egyptian. At some point, she became Sarah's servant, and later, at Sarah's command, Abraham's concubine. Although Hagar's status with regard to Abraham changed once she had been given to him, she remained Sarah's servant. The fact that trouble erupted is no surprise. The legal and ethical issues surrounding contemporary surrogate motherhood are complex and emotionally charged. They must have been all the more charged and complex in this ancient context.

Sarah's story is excerpted from a very long narrative extending from chapter 11 of Genesis through chapter 23. This section of Genesis also includes the

15

Akedah, *the binding and near-sacrifice of Isaac, Abraham and Sarah's longed-for, only son. Sarah is not mentioned in that account, although other aspects are mentioned in painstaking detail. The next chapter recounts Sarah's death at 127 years.*

As you read her tale, let a picture of Sarah emerge in your mind. How does the narrative itself view her? How does Abraham see her? How does she see herself? If she were to tell us her story, what do you think she would include—and leave out? What would you ask her?

Note carefully who speaks with God or God's messengers in this narrative and who does not. How does this influence your understanding of Hagar? How much of what occurs is the result of human action and how much of divine intervention?

~❦~

There was a famine in the land, and Abram went down to Egypt to sojourn there, for the famine was severe in the land. As he was about to enter Egypt, he said to his wife Sarai, "I know what a beautiful woman you are. If the Egyptians see you, and think, 'She is his wife,' they will kill me and let you live. Please say that you are my sister, that it may go well with me because of you, and that I may remain alive thanks to you."

When Abram entered Egypt, the Egyptians saw how very beautiful the woman was. Pharaoh's courtiers saw her and praised her to Pharaoh, and the woman was taken into Pharaoh's palace. And because of her, it went well with Abram; he acquired sheep, oxen, asses, male and female slaves, she-asses, and camels.

But the Lord afflicted Pharaoh and his household with mighty plagues on account of Sarai, the wife of Abram. Pharaoh sent for Abram and said, "What is this you have done to me! Why did you not tell me that she was your wife? Why did you say, 'She is my sister,' so that I took her as my wife? Now, here is your wife; take her and begone!" And Pharaoh put men in charge of him, and they sent him off with his wife and all that he possessed (Genesis 12:10–20).

. . . Sarai, Abram's wife, had borne him no children. She had an Egyptian maidservant whose name was Hagar. And Sarai said to Abram, "Look, the Lord has kept me from bearing. Consort with my maid; perhaps I shall have a son through her." And Abram heeded Sarai's request. So Sarai, Abram's wife, took her maid, Hagar the Egyptian—after Abram had dwelt in the land of Canaan ten years—and gave her to her husband Abram as concubine. He cohabited with Hagar and she conceived; and when she saw that she had conceived, her mistress was lowered in her esteem. And Sarai said to Abram, "The wrong done me is your fault! I myself put my maid in your bosom; now that she sees that she is pregnant, I am lowered in her esteem. The Lord decide between you and me!" Abram said to Sarai, "Your maid is in your hands. Deal with her as you think right." Then Sarai treated her harshly, and she ran away from her.

An angel of the Lord found her by a spring of water in the wilderness, the spring on the road to Shur, and said, "Hagar, slave of Sarai, where have you come from, and where are you going?" And she said, "I am running away from my mistress Sarai."

And the angel of the Lord said to her, "Go back your mistress, and submit to her harsh treatment." And the angel of the Lord said to her,

> "I will greatly increase your offspring,
> And they shall be too many to count."

The angel of the Lord said to her further,

> "Behold, you are with child
> And shall bear a son;
> You shall call him Ishmael,
> For the Lord has paid heed to your suffering.
> He shall be a wild ass of a man;
> His hand against everyone,
> And everyone's hand against him;
> He shall dwell alongside of all his kinsmen."

And she called the Lord who spoke to her, "You Are El-roi," by which she meant, "Have I not gone on seeing after He saw me!" Therefore the well was called Beer-lahai-roi; it is between Kadesh and Bered. . . . Hagar bore a son to Abram, and Abram gave the son that Hagar bore him the name of Ishmael. Abram was eighty-six years old when Hagar bore Ishmael to Abram. (Genesis 16:1–16).

. . . And God said to Abraham, "As for your wife Sarai, you shall not call her Sarai, but her name shall be Sarah. I will bless her; indeed, I will give you a son by her. I will bless her so that she shall give rise to nations; rulers of peoples shall issue from her." Abraham threw himself on his face and laughed, as he said to himself, "Can a child be born to a man a hundred years old, or can Sarah bear a child at ninety?" And Abraham said to God, "O that Ishmael might live by your favor!" God said, "Nevertheless, Sarah your wife shall bear you a son, and you shall name him Isaac; and I will maintain My covenant with him as an everlasting covenant for his offspring to come. As for Ishmael, I have heeded you. I hereby bless him. I will make him fertile and exceedingly numerous. He shall be the father of twelve chieftains, and I will make of him a great nation. But My covenant I will maintain with Isaac, whom Sarah shall bear to you at this season next year" (Genesis 17:15–21).

. . . The Lord appeared to him {Abraham} by the terebinths of Mamre; he was sitting at the entrance of the tent as the day grew hot. Looking up, he saw three men standing near him. As soon as he saw them, he ran from the entrance of the tent to greet them and, bowing to the ground, he said, "My lords, if it please you, do not go on past your servant. Let a little water be brought; bathe your feet and recline under the tree. And let me fetch a morsel of bread that you may refresh yourselves; then go on—seeing that you have come your servant's way." They replied, "Do as you have said."

Abraham hastened into the tent to Sarah, and said, "Quick, three *seahs* of choice flour! Knead and make cakes!" Then Abraham ran to the herd, took a calf, tender and choice, and gave it to a servant-boy, who hastened to prepare it. He took curds and milk and the calf that had been prepared and set these before them; and he waited on them under the tree as they ate.

They said to him, "Where is your wife Sarah?" And he replied, "There, in the tent." Then one said, "I will return to you next year, and your wife Sarah shall have a son!" Sarah was listening at the entrance of the tent, which was behind him. Now Abraham and Sarah were old, advanced in years; Sarah had stopped having the periods of women. And Sarah laughed to herself, saying, "Now that I am withered, am I to have enjoyment—with my husband so old?" Then the Lord said to Abraham, "Why did Sarah laugh, saying 'Shall I in truth bear a child, old as I am?' Is anything too wondrous for the Lord? I will return to you at the same season next year, and Sarah shall have a son." Sarah lied, saying "I did not laugh," for she was frightened. But He replied, "You did laugh" (Genesis 18:1–15).

. . . The Lord took note of Sarah as He had promised, and the Lord did for Sarah as He had spoken. Sarah conceived and bore a son to Abraham in his old age, at the set time of which God had spoken. Abraham gave his newborn son, whom Sarah had borne him, the name of Isaac. And when his son Isaac was eight days old, Abraham circumcised him, as God had commanded him. Now Abraham was a hundred years old when his son Isaac was born to him. Sarah said, "God has brought me laughter; everyone who hears will laugh with me." And she added,

> "Who would have said to Abraham
> That Sarah would suckle children!
> Yet I have borne a son in his old age."

The child grew up and was weaned, and Abraham held a great feast on the day that Isaac was weaned.

Sarah saw the son whom Hagar the Egyptian had borne to Abraham playing. She said to Abraham, "Cast out that slave-woman and her son, for the son of that slave shall not share in the inheritance with my son Isaac." The matter distressed Abraham greatly, for it concerned a son of his. But God said to Abraham, "Do not be distressed over the boy or your slave; whatever Sarah tells you, do as she says, for it is through Isaac that offspring shall be continued for you. As for the son of the slave-woman, I will make a nation of him, too, for he is your seed."

Early next morning Abraham took some bread and a skin of water, and gave them to Hagar. He placed them over her shoulder, together with the child, and sent her away. And she wandered about in the wilderness of Beer-sheba. When the water was gone from the skin, she left the child under one of the bushes, and went and sat down at a distance, a bowshot away; for she thought, "Let me not look on as the child dies." And sitting thus afar, she burst into tears.

God heard the cry of the boy, and an angel of God called to Hagar from heaven and said to her, "What troubles you, Hagar? Fear not, for God has heeded the cry of the boy where he is. Come, lift up the boy and hold him by the hand, for I will make a great nation of him." Then God opened her eyes and she saw a well of water. She went and filled the skin with water, and let the boy drink. God was with the boy and he grew up; he dwelt in the wilderness and became a bowman. He lived in the wilderness of Paran; and his mother got a wife for him from the land of Egypt. (Genesis 21:1–21).

. . . Sarah's lifetime—the span of Sarah's life—came to one hundred and twenty-seven years. Sarah died in Kiriath-arba—now Hebron—in the land of Canaan; and Abraham proceeded to mourn for Sarah and to bewail her. . . . And then Abraham buried his wife Sarah in the cave of the field of Machpelah, facing Mamre—now Hebron—in the land of Canaan (Genesis 23:1–3, 19).

Rabbinic Midrashim

As you will see below, the rabbinic tradition loves Sarah and bestows on her much praise. For what qualities do they praise her? Do you agree with their assessment? How do they view Hagar? Do you agree with that assessment? The Rabbis seem to focus on particular aspects of Sarah's life and ignore others. Why do you think they selected those incidents? On what parts of Sarah's life would you choose to comment?

God said to him: Here are many worlds for thee, as it is written, AND ABRAM TOOK SARAI HIS WIFE AND LOT HIS BROTHER'S SON AND ALL THEIR SUBSTANCE THAT THEY HAD GATHERED AND THE SOULS THAT THEY HAD MADE . . . IN HARAN [Genesis 12:5]. Now if all mankind come together in an endeavour to create one insect, they cannot do it; what it {the word "made"} means, therefore, is, the proselytes whom Abraham and Sarah converted. Therefore it is said, AND THE SOULS WHICH THEY HAD MADE IN HARAN. R. Ḥunia said: Abraham used to convert the men and Sarai the women.[1]

---

1. *Song of Songs Rabbah* 1:3, in *The Midrash*, ed. and trans. H. Freedman and Maurice Simon et al. (London: Soncino Press, 1951).

. . . When they arrived at the gate of Egypt, Abraham said to Sarah: My girl Egypt is a place of whoredom, as stated [Ezekiel 23:19–20]: . . . SHE WAS A WHORE IN THE LAND OF EGYPT, AND SHE LUSTED OVER THEIR PARAMOURS WHOSE FLESH IS LIKE THE FLESH OF ASSES. Let us, however, put you in a box and lock you in it. Then he did so. When they arrived at the gate of Egypt, the customs officers said to him: What are you carrying in the box? He said to them: Beans. They said to him: No, it is pepper. Give us the duty for pepper. He said to them: I shall hand it over. They said to him: It is not that. Rather, this box is full of gold coins. He said to them: I shall hand you over the duty for gold coins. When they saw that he was accepting whatever they would say about it, they said: Unless he had something of value in his possession, we [could] not be raising the price for him. At that moment, they said to him: You are not moving from here until you open the box. Then he said to them: It is up to me to give you whatever you want, but you are not to open the box. Nevertheless, they insisted on opening the box against his will and saw Sarah. When they saw her, they said: In the case of one like this, it is not seemly to touch her. Immediately they took [her] and brought her to Pharaoh. So they brought her into his palace. When Abraham saw that they had taken her and brought her unto Pharaoh, Abraham began to cry. [Sarah] also said: Sovereign of the World, Abraham came with you under a promise, since you had said to him [in Genesis 12:3]: I WILL BLESS THOSE WHO BLESS YOU. Now I did not know anything except that, when he told me that you had said to him [in Genesis 12:1] GO. I believed your words. But now, [when] I have been left isolated from my father, my mother, and my husband, this wicked man has come to mistreat me. He [Abraham] had acted because of your great name and because of our trust in your words. The Holy One said to her: By your life, nothing evil shall harm you, as stated [in Proverbs 12:21] NO HARM SHALL BEFALL THE RIGHTEOUS, BUT THE WICKED ARE FULL OF EVIL. So in regard to Pharaoh and his house, I will make an example of them. Thus it is written [in Genesis 12:17] THEN THE LORD AFFLICTED PHARAOH AND HIS HOUSE WITH GREAT PLAGUES AT THE WORD OF SARAI. In that very hour an angel came down from the heavens with a rod in his hand. [When] he came to touch her clothes, he would smite him. And the angel would consult with Sarah on each and every blow. If she said that he should be afflicted, he was afflicted. When she would say: Wait for him until he recovers himself, the angel would wait for him, as stated [in Genesis 12:17]: AT THE WORD OF SARAI.[2]

THAT SARAH SHOULD HAVE GIVEN CHILDREN SUCK [Genesis 21:7]. She suckled builders {reading *banim*, children, as *banaim*, builders}. Our mother Sarah was extremely modest. Said Abraham to her: "This is not a time for modesty, but uncover your breasts so that all may know that the Holy One, Blessed be He, has begun to perform miracles." She uncovered her breasts, and the milk gushed forth as from two fountains, and noble ladies came and had their children suckled by her, saying, "We do not merit that our children should be suckled with the milk of that righteous woman." The Rabbis said: Whoever came for the sake of heaven became God-fearing.[3]

. . . When Isaac returned to his mother, she asked him, "Where have you been, my son?" He answered her, "Father took me, led me up mountains and down valleys, took me up a certain mountain, built an altar, arranged the wood, bound me upon it, and took hold of a knife to slay me. If an angel had not come from heaven and said to him, 'ABRAHAM, ABRAHAM, LAY NOT THY HAND UPON THE LAD' [Genesis 22:11–12], I should have been slain." On his mother, Sarah, hearing this, she cried out, and before she had time to finish her cry her soul departed, as it is written, AND ABRAHAM CAME TO MOURN FOR SARAH AND TO WEEP FOR HER [ibid., 23:2]. From where did he come? From Mount Moriah {the mountain where he was to sacrifice Isaac}.[4]

R. Simeon b. Yoḥai said: Hagar was Pharaoh's daughter. When Pharaoh saw what was done on Sarah's behalf in his own house, he took his daughter and gave her to Sarah, saying, "Better let my daughter be a

2. *Midrash Tanhuma* 3:8, in *Midrash Tanhuman*, trans. John T. Townsend (Hoboken, NJ: Ktav Publishing House, 1989).

3. *Genesis Rabbah* 53:9, in *The Midrash*, ed. and trans. H. Freedman and Maurice Simon et al. (London: Soncino Press, 1951).

4. *Ecclesiastes Rabbah* 9:7, in ibid.

handmaid in this house than a mistress in another house"; thus it is written, AND SHE HAD A HANDMAID, AN EGYPTIAN, WHOSE NAME WAS HAGAR [Genesis 16:1], he [Pharaoh] saying, "Here is thy reward (*agar*)."[5]

Ladies used to come and inquire how she {Sarah} was, and she would say to them, "Go and ask about the welfare of this poor woman [Hagar]." Hagar would tell them: "My mistress Sarai is not inwardly what she is outwardly: She appears to be a righteous woman, but she is not. For had she been a righteous woman, see how many years have passed without her conceiving, whereas I conceived in one night!"[6]

God's Covenant with Sarah

by Karen Prager

Karen Prager's story of the relationship between Sarah and Hagar gives voice to the idea that the personal is the political. How does her account differ from the biblical narrative, and how is it the same? How does her vision of Sarah compare to that of the Rabbis?

Commentary: God speaks to Hagar and God speaks to Sarah in Genesis 15–18. In this story, Hagar and Sarah give voice to their longings. Sarah tells us how she came to understand herself, and how she made peace with Hagar, with herself, and with God.

Sarai and Abram dwelled with Mamre the Amorite; Abram's nephew Lot lived in Sodom. One morning Abram came to Sarai and said, "God has granted me another vision. Our land surrounds us! We shall be buried here in peace. But there is more. You and I shall have a child!" Sarai turned to the valley with wistful gaze. She said, "You and I are old now.

---

5. *Genesis Rabbah* 45:1, in ibid.
6. *Genesis Rabbah* 45:4, in ibid.

Your black hair is ribboned white, and my eyes speak of sunshine and laughter. God makes me no such promises."

Hagar was indentured to Abram in Egypt while Sarai lived with Pharaoh. Hagar was poor; her family was of lowly status. Hagar was not a free woman. Her survival lay in her travels with the family from Haran. Sarai thought, "Why not let Hagar bear an heir for our fortune?" Hagar did as Sarai said, and was Abram's concubine until she became pregnant.

Sarai spoke to Hagar and said, "Do you think you are better for Abram than I because you are pregnant with his child?" Hagar spoke back, "I am your servant; I endure your aging husband at your bidding. Do you now begrudge Hagar her only child?" Sarai cried, "I grieve for the child I never had. Your belly affronts me; it taunts my loss." Hagar intoned, "What loving husband have I with whom to share an infant? I give birth alone, in the shadow of your anger. Once born, my child will have your inheritance. What will he know of Hagar's ancestors? What will he know of Egypt?"

Sarai said bitterly, "In Egypt I hated my husband. Now I hate you. Get out of my sight."

In fear and in fury, Hagar left their encampment. On the road to Shur, near a spring of water, Hagar gave birth to a son, Ishmael. And behold! An angel of God came to her. The angel was comely, with tawny hair. He spoke softly, "Where are you going, Hagar?" Hagar cried and laughed. "I have a beautiful son. Who will love him but I?" The angel said, "Your love is more powerful than the Amorite army. Ishmael will father a dark and mighty people. Return and find a sister in Sarai. Raise your child with the Hebrew family." The angel quenched Hagar's thirst, and she returned to Sarai.

While Hagar wandered, Sarai sought God. God sent three angels. Abram bathed their feet; Sarai made them cakes. The angels promised them, "You will yet have a son." Sarai found laughter, saying, "Now I am withered! Am I to have enjoyment with this old man, my husband?" Then God spoke to them and chided, "You think you know what is to come? For time everlasting I will maintain my covenant with your child. As many stars as are in the sky, that is how many your people will number. I will make of your son a great nation."

Then God named them Sarah and Abraham, the parents of a nation. As God had promised, Sarah became pregnant. In her joy and shame, she again sought God's counsel. "God, I have wronged another woman with what I have demanded. How can I deserve Your benevolence?" God said, "I made woman in My image. As you are, so is Hagar. If you speak to her, she will tell you the gifts you may offer her." So God sent Sarah back to Hagar, whom she met carrying Ishmael, returning to camp.

Sarah cried to Hagar, "Must it always be so? As was done to me I must do? My sexuality was an Egyptian pharaoh's plaything, and long my hate and anger remained. I know the sorrow of lying with a man I do not love, yet here I have made such a bed for you! Tell me how I may I heal this wrong."

Hagar said, "Let Ishmael and Isaac grow up as brothers. Each shall have two mothers and one father. You alone shall be my family. Together we will teach our children about the God we have found. Your child shall have his inheritance. Ishmael will know his homeland through our stories, and will return to Egypt to build a nation."

This is how Hagar and Sarah came to raise the ancestors of two great nations. In time, Hagar and Ishmael went south to reclaim their land. God attended to their journey with Her love.

From "The Death of Sarah"

by Susan Gross

Causing a woman to give birth at ninety is certainly within God's power, but can Sarah cope with it? Susan Gross's evocative description of an aged Sarah contemplating this eventuality asks that question. Do you see it the same way? How does this portrayal of Sarah compare to those of Karen Prager and Ellen Umansky?

Sarah tore stringy green husks away from the new-white pole beans. Halfway through the job she took the bean basket from between her legs, set it down on the red earth, and kneaded the joints of her fingers. Then she ran her hands through her white hair, slowly. Her fingers ached.

She drew her head around in a wide arc to get the kinks out of her neck. As she brought her face forward again she glimpsed tiny cyclones of dust rising on the horizon. She squinted, but that only made her vision worse. Who was it? she thought with a small swelling of fear.

After a few minutes she could see three figures: three men walking in lockstep rhythm, advancing at jackal-speed. Sarah looked at Abraham whose attention, too, was fixed on the approaching strangers. But a subtle smile toyed with his lips. "Food for the guests!" he ordered. The servants who were lounged outside the tents suddenly spun into activity. Sarah sighed. Then she pushed herself off of her chair and stood, her joints still throbbing.

She went behind the circle of tents and helped pound cake dough. She threw her round cakes onto the fire hood and watched as they blistered. The smoke stung her eyes. She wanted to wait until the cakes were done so she could serve them to the visitors. That way she could get a clear look at them. But the heat of the fire and the insistent smoke stole her strength. She had to lie down. If she didn't find her tent immediately she might faint. . . .

Sarah tottered and put out her arms. She caught the shoulder of one of the maids' children. It was Ishmael, with his round face and fuzzy, short hair. He let her put her weight on him, and they walked to Sarah's tent. He held the flap open for her but wouldn't step over the threshold.

"Thank you," she coughed. She stretched out her legs and lay with her head propped on two pillows.

"Just rest, Grandmother," he called softly. Then he let the door flap drop. Sarah heard him scamper away.

His name for her rang between her ears. They all called her Grandmother, all of the servants' children, though she wasn't truly anyone's grandmother, or mother. That dream had died ages ago. . . .

She drifted to sleep.

When she woke she heard laughter, her own. She had been dreaming a bright dream with red flowers and noisy children. There had been babies in her lap, bouncing and burping. . . . The laughter vanished as soon as she realized fully that it had been only a dream. She looked around the dim tent. She saw her wrinkled knees lying, coffin-like, before her. She heard her own breath rattle within her lungs.

How dreadful it would be to have a child now, she thought. She imagined a great heaviness in her womb, so heavy that she was paralyzed under it. She imagined chasing after a child: he darting on thick pink legs and she hobbling, never catching him, sinking into her grave. Sarah tried to get up. As she wrestled herself to a sitting position, she heard voices: deep male voices, not far away.

It was the guests. Sarah slowly made her way to the tent flap and peered out. She could see Abraham sitting beneath a shade tree. The three strange men sat cross-legged around him.

Abraham noticed her. He wagged his finger at her playfully. Sarah elaborately furrowed her brow to tell him she didn't understand what he meant by that gesture. She emerged from her tent. The other men stood up and stared at her.

She walked toward them. They were only a few feet away, but it seemed to her that she took forever to reach them. Finally she stood beside one of the strangers. Her head only came up to his breastbone. She looked up at his face and was startled by its purity. There were no wrinkles, no leathery sun-streaks, no marks of age. And yet he was not a youth. Too much wisdom was in his eyes. She looked at the other two strangers and found the same features. Then her gaze settled on Abraham, whose countenance was shriveled and whose eyes were smokey.

"You laughed," Abraham said to her. There was an accusing tone in his voice. The other men nodded.

"No. Did I? Oh, it was just a dream. I was napping, I think."

"You must have heard us, and you laughed," Abraham insisted.

"You did laugh, but you must believe us," the stranger next to her said. "You *will* bear."

Sarah had never heard such a deep voice. It didn't sound human. The fear that had swelled earlier returned and grew larger. Bear what? she wondered. She stood there silently, trying to pick up a clue from the presence of these strange strangers. Sometimes she could understand that way: by urging information out of the air, not using her senses, just letting it flow in. It could be called a kind of prophecy. In the space of a few seconds she had it. The man meant a child. She would bear a child. Pinpoints of pain scurried up her legs, and she lurched into Abraham's arms.

The next thing she knew, she was sitting against the trunk of the shade tree. Abraham and his friends had moved some paces away. They spoke to each other in low tones. Then they raised their hands in farewell. The strangers retreated in the direction they had come, and Abraham pivoted to face her.

Sarah swatted tears on her cheek. "How gruesome! How could they take advantage of your hospitality? How could they play such a queer joke on two old souls?"

He sat down with her. "They meant well. They mean to bless us, Sarah; it's wonderful news. It isn't a joke at all."

"I know it isn't!" she screeched.

"Why are you upset? Isn't this what we've always prayed for?"

"Not now. Not anymore. I'm so tired. If they had announced that I were dying, I would be overjoyed."

"Sarah." He seemed to deflate.

"Let's move. Let's go somewhere else, so those men will never find us again."

"We will. But what will that solve? We take our bodies with us. Your womb, your life . . ." He breathed in. He put his arms around her hunched shoulders and squeezed her with certain strength. The air intoxicated him. "It's wonderful news," he repeated.

They broke camp the next day. Sarah moved through the motions with limbs of stone. Someone lifted her onto a donkey. A thought sprung up in her mind and attached itself to the lazy gait of the beast: I want to die, I want to die, I want to die. . . . She wouldn't look at anyone. Instead, she concentrated on the ghost-like heat vapor in the distance.

Re-Visioning Sarah: A Midrash on Genesis 22
by Ellen M. Umansky

The Rabbis connect Sarah's death with Isaac's near-sacrifice, but Ellen Umansky reflects on Sarah's reaction to the knowledge that her husband would do even this. Does the biblical account give us any clues about Sarah's relationship with Abraham? What do you think of this interpretation?

It was morning. Sarah had just awakened and reached over to touch her husband, Abraham, to caress him, but Abraham wasn't there. Neither, she discovered, was Isaac, her only son, Isaac, whom she loved more than anyone or anything in the world. She quickly dressed and went outside, hoping they'd be nearby. But they were gone, and so was Abraham's ass and his two young servants. It wasn't unusual for Abraham to take Isaac somewhere, but never this early and never without saying goodbye. And so she waited, and wept, and screamed.

Hours passed. It was hot and Sarah thought about going inside to escape the heat of the sun. But what if I miss them, she thought. I want to make sure that I catch the first glimpse of them, even if they're far away. And so she stood and waited . . . and waited . . . and waited. She felt anxious, nervous, upset. "Where could they be?" "Where has Abraham taken my son?" The sun began to set. She started to shiver, partly from the cold, mostly from fear. Again she cried, and wailed, and moaned. Isaac had been God's gift to her, a sign of His love and a continuing bond between them. She had laughed when God told her she was pregnant. She was old and no longer able to bear a child. But God had given her Isaac and filled her breasts with milk and for the first time in her life Sarah was happy.

She looked around her and saw the fields, now empty, and in the distance saw the mountains, sloping upwards into the sky. And then she saw them . . . Abraham walking with his ass and his servants and Isaac far behind, walking slowly, his head turning from side to side, his hands oddly moving as though he were trying to make sense of something; and Sarah knew in that instant where Abraham and Isaac had been and why they had gone. Though she could barely make out the features of Isaac's face, she could tell from his movements and his gestures that he was angry, that he wanted nothing to do with his father who had tried to kill him. Abraham was almost down the mountain by now and soon would be home. He'd try to explain, to make her understand *his* side of the story. But Sarah wanted no part of it. She was tired of hearing Abraham's excuses and even more tired of hearing what *he* thought God demanded. And so Sarah turned and went inside and prayed that if only for one night, Abraham would leave her alone.

3

LOT'S WIFE AND DAUGHTERS

Lot's Wife and Daughters in the Bible

When Abraham heard of God's intention to destroy Sodom and Gomorrah because of the unmitigated sinfulness of the residents, he begged God not to destroy the innocent along with the guilty. God agreed that if ten innocent people were found, the city would be spared for their sake. As you will read, only Lot, his wife, and two of their daughters were saved.

Lot was Abraham's nephew. He left Haran with Abraham and Sarah, and later settled in Sodom. His wife and daughters are not named, and very little is said about them. Do you think Lot should have been rescued? Why do you think Lot's wife and daughters are nameless? Why do you think Lot's wife was punished? How do you understand the conclusion of the narrative?

The two angels arrived in Sodom in the evening, as Lot was sitting in the gate of Sodom. When Lot saw them, he rose to greet them and, bowing low with his face to the ground, he said, "Please, my lords, turn aside to your servant's house to spend the night, and bathe your feet; then you may be on your way early." But they said, "No, we will spend the night in the square." But he urged them strongly, so they turned his way and entered his house. He prepared a feast for them and baked unleavened bread, and they ate.

They had not yet lain down, when the townspeople, the men of Sodom, young and old—all the people to the last man—gathered about the house. And they shouted to Lot and said to him, "Where are the men who came to you tonight? Bring them out to us, that we may be intimate with them." So Lot went out to them to the entrance, shut the door behind him, and said, "I beg you, my friends, do not commit such a wrong. Look, I have two daughters who have not known a man. Let me bring them out to you, and you may do to them as you please; but do not do anything to these men, since they have come under the shelter of my roof." But they said, "Stand back! The fellow," they said, "came here as an alien, and already he acts the ruler! Now we will deal worse with you than with them." And they pressed hard against the person of Lot, and moved forward to break the door. But the men stretched out their hands and pulled Lot into the house with them, and shut the door. And the people who were at the entrance of the house, young and old, were struck with blinding light, so that they were helpless to find the entrance.

Then the men said to Lot, "Whom else have you here? Sons-in-law, your sons and daughters, or anyone else that you have in the city—bring them out of the place. For we are about to destroy this place; because the outcry against them before the Lord has become so great that the Lord has sent us to destroy it." So Lot went out and spoke to his sons-in-law, who had married his daughters, and said, "Up, get out of this place, for the Lord is about to destroy the city." But he seemed to his sons-in-law as one who jests.

As dawn broke, the angels urged Lot on, saying, "Up, take your wife and your two remaining daughters, lest you be swept away because of the iniquity of the city." Still he delayed. So the men seized his hand, and the hands of his wife and daughters—in the Lord's mercy on him—and brought him out and left him outside the city. When they had brought them outside, one said, "Flee for your life! Do not look behind you, nor stop anywhere in the Plain; flee to the hills, lest you be swept away." But Lot said to them, "Oh no, my lord! You have been so gracious to your servant, and have already shown me so much kindness in order to save my life; but I cannot flee to the hills, lest the disaster overtake me and I die. Look, that town there is near enough to flee to; it is such a little place! Let me flee there—it is such a little place—and let my life be saved." He replied, "Very well, I will grant you this favor too, and I will not annihilate the town of which you have spoken. Hurry, flee there, for I cannot do anything until you arrive there." Hence the town came to be called Zoar.

As the sun rose upon the earth and Lot entered Zoar, the Lord rained upon Sodom and Gomorrah sulfurous fire from the Lord out of heaven. He annihilated those cities and the entire Plain, and all the inhabitants of the cities and the vegetation of the ground. Lot's wife looked back, and she thereupon turned into a pillar of salt.

Next morning, Abraham hurried to the place where he had stood before the Lord, and, looking down toward Sodom and Gomorrah and all the land of the Plain, he saw the smoke of the land rising like the smoke of a kiln.

Thus it was that, when God destroyed the cities of the Plain and annihilated the cities where Lot dwelt, God was mindful of Abraham and removed Lot from the midst of the upheaval.

Lot went up from Zoar and settled in the hill country with his two daughters, for he was afraid to dwell in Zoar; and he and his two daughters lived in a cave. And the older one said to the younger, "Our father is old, and there is not a man on earth to consort with us in the way of all the world. Come, let us make our father drink wine, and let us lie with him, that we may maintain life through our father." That night they made their father drink wine, and the older one went in and lay with her father; he did not know when she lay down or when she rose. The next day the older one said to the younger, "See, I lay with Father last night; let us make him drink wine tonight also, and you go and lie with him, that we may maintain life through our father." That night also they made their father drink wine, and the younger one went and lay with him; he did not know when she lay down or when she rose.

Thus the two daughters of Lot came to be with child by their father. The older one bore a son and named him Moab; he is the father of the Moabites of today. And the younger also bore a son, and she called him Ben-ammi; he is the father of the Ammonites of today (Genesis 19).

Rabbinic Midrashim

There is much that is troubling in the story of Sodom and Gomorrah. The first midrash seeks to explain Sodom's fate and also gives a name to one of Lot's daughters. In the second midrash, the Rabbis seem to be assuming that looking back was an insufficient sin to warrant such an extreme and unusual punishment. Do you agree? They also try to explain why Lot's wife was turned into a pillar of salt. What are the issues or aspects of the story that drew you in? Do the Rabbis share your concerns?

Rabbi Judah said: It was proclaimed in Sodom, "He who sustains a stranger or a poor and needy person with a morsel of bread is to be burned alive."

Lot's daughter, Pelotit, was married to one of Sodom's notables. Seeing a poor man languishing in the town square, she felt sorry for him. What did she do? Every day when she went down to draw water, she would put into her pitcher some of every kind of food she had in her house, and thus sustained the poor man. The people of Sodom kept wondering: How does this poor man manage to stay alive? Finally they figured out the reason, and they brought Pelotit out to be burned.

She prayed, "God of the universe, exact justice and judgment in my behalf from the Sodomites." Her cry rose up before the throne of glory. The Holy One said, "I will go down and see whether they have done according to her cry" (Genesis 18:21)—if the people of Sodom have indeed done according to the cry of this young woman, I will turn the city's foundations over to the top and the city's top to the bottom.[1]

BUT HIS WIFE LOOKED BACK FROM BEHIND HIM, AND SHE BECAME A PILLAR OF SALT (Genesis 19:26)—because R. Isaac said, she sinned through salt. On the night that the angels visited Lot,

---

1. Pirke de-Rabbi Eliezer, in *The Book of Legends*, ed. Hayim Nahman Bialik and Yehoshua Hana Ravnitzky; trans. William G. Braude (New York: Schocken Books, 1992).

Lot said to his wife, "Give these guests a bit of salt." But she replied, "[Besides entertaining guests], is it your wish to introduce into Sodom another vile custom [that of seasoning their food]?" What did she do? She went around among all her neighbors saying to each, "Give me salt—we have guests," intending thereby to have the townspeople become aware of the presence of guests in her home [and penalize Lot for it]. Hence, SHE HERSELF BECAME A PILLAR OF SALT (ibid.).[2]

This is Lot's wife, Edith, of whom it is stated (in Genesis 19:26): BUT HIS WIFE LOOKED BACK, AND SHE BECAME A PILLAR OF SALT.[3]

The Cave

by Alicia Suskin Ostriker

Many contemporary commentators, both male and female, seem to be drawn to the question of why Lot's wife looked back. Alicia Suskin Ostriker turns her attention to the equally troubling issue of the incestuous rape of Lot by his daughters. Is this the issue you would have addressed? Do you agree with this interpretation?

> *Come, let us make our father drink wine, and we will lie with him, that we may preserve the seed of the father.*
>
> Genesis 19:32

> *Cave girl mama*
> *Don't you go down on me.*
> *Oh cave girl mama*
> *Don't you go down on me.*
> *Take your pretty legs and your tangled hair*
> *Away and just leave me be.*

---

2. *Genesis Rabbah* 51:5, 50:4, ibid.

3. *Midrash Tanhuma* 4:8, in *Midrash Tanhuman*, trans. John T. Townsend (Hoboken, NJ: Ktav Publishing House, 1989). This name alludes to the Hebrew word 'ed, meaning witness.

"What is a cave, and how deep must it go?" they must have wondered. The girls, they were really women, the daughters, the daughters of their father. They had never known a man. You remember the daughters. The first important ones. Daughters of Lot, nieces of Abraham, temporary inhabitants of Sodom, a city of the plain which is no longer in existence. They themselves had not looked back, unlike their mother. Unlike, unlike. Unlike who? Long afterward they might have hung on a ledge, peering, back there, at the widths of the flat landscape, so difficult really to discern anything, a mineral formation, back there, a mineral formation in the middle of what was flat and burnt-out, really, standing up it could have been white and salty, it could have been shaped like a pillar, only it was difficult, really, to see anything.

The hawks, they spiral. I wish I could be like them. Blindingly cruel, the floating, on the airdrafts, far below one's feet, gradually ascending until you can distinguish the feathers at the wing-ends dipping, lightly, to steer them. Now time goes by, I'm hypnotized by the breeze. And then when they drop, it is just like a thunderbolt, the talons come out, the beak widens, it is over in a minute. The killing is over in a minute, a swift crunch, a swallow, and the gliding begins again, the volumes of space, the shadowy cliff, the hypnosis.

A holocaust is unlike this. Unlike, unlike. For example, it takes much longer. It is much louder. It stinks worse. It is much more redness. Far, far more redness (How do the girls know, if they don't see it? If they obey and don't look back? They still know. How could they fail to know. Perhaps they know by the heat, perhaps by the roar. For everyone has heard a fire roaring, and felt the terrifying heat when you come too close, that whips at your back even when you are running away, until you are finally to freshness). While you are running away it is going on, on, on.

Afterward the smoke of the country goes up like smoke from furnace.

A cave mouth. You go inside the mouth, it becomes cool, it can be comfortable, it can be home. Deep in, here you are, fix it up, girls. You have to be hiding. You have to keep on hiding here. But why?

They were wicked people. But is it true that the girls can never go back, can never in fact leave these cliffs where they are hiding out, and this cave here? The cities were all full of wicked people, so the girls must not (they do not) remember the girls who used to be their friends, or the mothers of those girls. They must not (do not) think about their clothing, their jewelry, or their makeup. Bad girls. Bad mothers. Now they are cinders.

Innocence means: we have never known a man. Father says: we are good girls. He tries to pet our heads but his hand slides over the fronts of our faces. It is like having a blind person touch you. He cries all of the time. It is disgusting.

Innocence means: we do not remember the night the two men were staying at our house, the night the drunken crowd was roaring outside our door (we used to see them in daytime, our girlfriends' fathers, brothers, and uncles) banging at the windows (wanting to fuck our visitors), the night our father took us by the elbows and tried to push us outside the door instead. He thought we might be a substitute, and yelled through the door that they should do whatever they wanted with us. He was pulling one way, we were pulling the other, screaming our heads off. Our mother was screaming, hitting him, trying to get his face with her nails. Innocence means we do not remember our mother.

Here we are in the cave. Cool and nice, cool and safe. Some of the rocks look like dragons and some like camels, we eat over here and sleep over here, using skins. But he cries all of the time and it is disgusting. Tears and snot and dribble mingling on his face. We ask him about husbands. Where is he going to find us husbands, because we have to have children. But he dribbles and bawls, and it is really disgusting. Also, he gets drunk every night.

It is easy to get him drunk.

Now it is easy, when he is drunk and asleep. We are giggling for days beforehand. You go first. No, you.

Oily, I've used the fat of a wildcat I skinned. Candle steady, shadows on his nipples he's sound asleep, I can look him over head to knees. Unlike, unlike. Unlike ourselves, less soft but more meaty. I circle the dove brown aureoles with my index finger, skim lightly by the hairs until the nipples harden like snaps. I use my tongue tip and, very carefully, my teeth. I crouch until my breasts flap against his face like hot towels. The air grows denser and the room heats from the single candle's brilliant orange cone, edged gold, diffused to smoke lifted like a string. His red body resembles clay, which invites the fingers to burrow in. I pursue the rivulets of his fur down the center, downstream, I make it wet and greasy,

I make it shine. Now here is his baby thing, a sleepy puppy. Now here we go, a dog sitting up begging. Oh my mama I'm happy filling up my mouth with figs, another breast, the blissful childhood I can't remember. And slip now and slide. Mama, no giggling. A gush of blood, but it feels good. God, it feels finally good.

First me then her. Tomorrow her then me.

Do you guess he was only pretending to be asleep, on the ledge, the skins, the leaves, in the warm room in the cave.

Cave girl Mama
Go put your red dress on
Yeah Cave Girl Mama
Go put your red dress on
Put some lipstick on your mouth and we'll
Cakewalk into town.

4

REBEKAH

Rebekah in the Bible

Rebekah is the middle Matriarch, who was joined to Sarah and Abraham's son, Isaac. As you read the story of their life together, compare their roles in both their marriage and the birthright deception. Why do you think God revealed their sons' futures to her and not to Isaac? What adjectives would you use to describe Rebekah—Isaac? Note the instances in which she takes action and their context.

When Rebekah first sees Isaac, our translation tells us that "she alighted from the camel" (Genesis 24:64). One translation suggests that "she inclined while upon the camel."[1] The Hebrew itself is ambiguous, permitting either of these interpretations as well as the reading that she literally fell off of the camel. What do you think?

~❦~

Abraham was now old, advanced in years, and the Lord had blessed Abraham in all things. And Abraham said to the senior servant of his

------

1. Nosson, Scherman, *The Chumash* (Brooklyn, NY: Mesorah Publications 1993), p. 121.

household, who had charge of all that he owned, "Put your hand under my thigh and I will make you swear by the Lord, the God of heaven and the God of the earth, that you will not take a wife for my son from the daughters of the Canaanites among whom I dwell, but will go to the land of my birth and get a wife for my son Isaac." And the servant said to him, "What if the woman does not consent to follow me to this land, shall I then take your son back to the land from which you came?" Abraham answered him, "On no account must you take my son back there! The Lord, the God of heaven, who took me from my father's house and from my native land, who promised me on oath, saying, 'I will assign this land to your offspring'—He will send His angel before you, and you will get a wife for my son from there. And if the woman does not consent to follow you, you shall then be clear of this oath to me; but do not take my son back there." So the servant put his hand under the thigh of his master Abraham and swore to him as bidden.

Then the servant took ten of his master's camels and set out, taking with him all the bounty of his master; and he made his way to Aram-naharim, to the city of Nahor. He made the camels kneel down by the well outside the city, at evening time, the time when women come out to draw water. And he said, "O Lord, God of my master Abraham, grant me good fortune this day, and deal graciously with my master Abraham: Here I stand by the spring as the daughters of the townsmen come out to draw water; let the maiden to whom I say, 'Please, lower your jar that I may drink,' and who replies, 'Drink, and I will also water your camels'—let her be the one whom You have decreed for your servant Isaac. Thereby shall I know that You have dealt graciously with my master."

He had scarcely finished speaking, when Rebekah, who was born to Bethuel, the son of Milcah the wife of Abraham's brother Nahor, came out with her jar on her shoulder. The maiden was very beautiful, a virgin whom no man had known. She went down to the spring, filled her jar, and came up. The servant ran toward her and said, "Please, let me sip a little water from your jar." "Drink, my lord," she said, and she quickly lowered her jar upon her hand and let him drink. When she had let him drink his fill, she said, "I will also draw for your camels, until they finish drinking." Quickly emptying her jar into the trough, she ran back to the well to draw, and she drew for all his camels.

The man, meanwhile, stood gazing at her, silently wondering whether the Lord had made his errand successful or not. When the camels had finished drinking, the man took a gold nose-ring weighing a half-shekel, and two gold bands for her arms, ten shekels in weight. "Pray tell me," he said, "whose daughter are you? Is there room in your father's house for us to spend the night?" She replied, "I am the daughter of Bethuel the son of Milcah, whom she bore to Nahor." And she went on, "There is plenty of straw and feed at home, and also room to spend the night." The man bowed low in homage to the Lord and said, "Blessed be the Lord, the God of my master Abraham, who has not withheld His steadfast faithfulness from my master. For I have been guided on my errand by the Lord, to the house of my master's kinsmen."

The maiden ran and told all this to her mother's household. Now Rebekah had a brother whose name was Laban. Laban ran out to the man at the spring—when he saw the nose-ring and the bands on his sister's arms, and when he heard his sister Rebekah say, "Thus the man spoke to me." He went up to the man, who was still standing beside the camels at the spring. "Come in, O blessed of the Lord," he said, "why do you remain outside, when I have made ready the house, and a place for the camels?" So the man entered the house, and the camels were unloaded. The camels were given straw and feed, and water was brought to bathe his feet and the feet of the men with him. But when the food was set before him, he said, "I will not eat until I have told my tale." He said, "Speak then."

"I am Abraham's servant," he began. "The Lord has greatly blessed my master, and he has become rich: He has given him sheep and cattle, silver and gold, male and female slaves, camels and asses. And Sarah, my master's wife, bore my master a son in her old age, and he has assigned to him everything he owns. Now my master made me swear, saying, 'You shall not get a wife for my son from the daughters of the Canaanites in whose land I dwell; but you shall go to my father's house, to my kindred, and get a wife for my son.' And I said to my master, 'What if the woman does not follow me?' He replied to me, 'The Lord, whose ways I have followed, will send His angel with you and make your errand successful; and you will get a wife for my son from my kindred, from my father's house. Thus only shall you be freed from my adjuration: if, when you come to my kindred, they refuse you—only then shall you be freed from my adjuration.'

"I came to the spring, and I said: 'O Lord, God of my master Abraham, if You would indeed grant success to the errand on which I am engaged! As I stand by the spring of water, let the young woman who comes out to draw and to whom I say, "Please, let me drink a little water from your jar," and who answers, "You may drink, and I will also draw for your camels"—let her be the wife whom the Lord has decreed for my master's son.' I had scarcely finished praying in my heart, when Rebekah came out with her jar on her shoulder, and went down to the spring and drew. And I said to her, 'Please give me a drink.' She quickly lowered her jar and said, 'Drink, and I will also water your camels.' So I drank, and she also watered the camels. I inquired of her, 'Whose daughter are you?' And she said, 'The daughter of Bethuel, son of Nahor, whom Milcah bore to him.' And I put the ring on her nose and the bands on her arms. Then I bowed low in homage to the Lord and blessed the Lord, the God of my master Abraham, who led me on the right way to get the daughter of my master's brother for his son. And now, if you mean to treat my master with true kindness, tell me; and if not, tell me also, that I may turn right or left."

Then Laban and Bethuel answered, "The matter was decreed by the Lord; we cannot speak to you bad or good. Here is Rebekah before you; take her and go, and let her be a wife to your master's son, as the Lord has spoken." When Abraham's servant heard their words, he bowed low to the ground before the Lord. The servant brought out objects of silver and gold, and garments, and gave them to Rebekah; and he gave presents to her brother and her mother. Then he and the men with him ate and drank, and they spent the night. When they arose next morning, he said, "Give me leave to go to my master." But her brother and her mother said, "Let the maiden remain with us some ten days; then you may go." He said to them, "Do not delay me, now that the Lord has made my errand successful. Give me leave that I may go to my master." And they said, "Let us call the girl and ask for her reply." They called Rebekah and said to her, "Will you go with this man?" And she said, "I will." So they sent off their sister Rebekah and her nurse along with Abraham's servant and his men. And they blessed Rebekah and said to her,

"O sister!
May you grow

> Into thousands of myriads;
> May your offspring seize
> The gates of their foes."

Then Rebekah and her maids arose, mounted the camels, and followed the man. So the servant took Rebekah and went his way.

Isaac had just come back from the vicinity of Beer-lahai-roi, for he was settled in the region of the Negeb. And Isaac went out walking in the field toward evening and, looking up, he saw camels approaching. Raising her eyes, Rebekah saw Isaac. She alighted from the camel and said to the servant, "Who is that man walking in the field toward us?" And the servant said, "That is my master." So she took her veil and covered herself. The servant told Isaac all the things that he had done. Isaac then brought her into the tent of his mother Sarah, and he took Rebekah as his wife. Isaac loved her, and thus found comfort after his mother's death (Genesis 24:1–67).

. . . This is the story of Isaac, son of Abraham. Abraham begot Isaac. Isaac was forty years old when he took to wife Rebekah, daughter of Bethuel the Aramean of Paddan-aram, sister of Laban the Aramean. Isaac pleaded with the Lord on behalf of his wife, because she was barren; and the Lord responded to his plea, and his wife Rebekah conceived. But the children struggled in her womb, and she said, "If so, why do I exist?" She went to inquire of the Lord, and the Lord answered her,

> "Two nations are in your womb,
> Two separate peoples shall issue from your body;
> One people shall be mightier than the other,
> And the older shall serve the younger."

When her time to give birth was at hand, there were twins in her womb. The first one emerged red, like a hairy mantle all over; so they named him Esau. Then his brother emerged, holding on to the heel of Esau; so they named him Jacob. Isaac was sixty years old when they were born.

When the boys grew up, Esau became a skillful hunter, a man of the outdoors; but Jacob was a mild man who stayed in camp. Isaac favored Esau because he had a taste for game; but Rebekah favored Jacob (Genesis 25:19–28).

. . . When Isaac was old and his eyes were too dim to see, he called his older son Esau and said to him, "My son." He answered, "Here I am." And he said, "I am old now, and I do not know how soon I may die. Take your gear, your quiver and bow, and go out into the open and hunt me some game. Then prepare a dish for me such as I like, and bring it to me to eat, so that I may give you my innermost blessing before I die."

Rebekah had been listening as Isaac spoke to his son Esau. When Esau had gone out into the open to hunt game to bring home, Rebekah said to her son Jacob, "I overheard your father speaking to your brother Esau, saying, 'Bring me some game and prepare a dish for me to eat, that I may bless you, with the Lord's approval, before I die.' Now, my son, listen carefully as I instruct you. Go to the flock and fetch me two choice kids, and I will make of them a dish for your father, such as he likes. Then take it to your father to eat, in order that he may bless you before he dies." Jacob answered his mother Rebekah, "But my brother Esau is a hairy man and I am smooth-skinned. If my father touches me, I shall appear to him as a trickster and bring upon myself a curse, not a blessing." But his mother said to him, "Your curse, my son, be upon me! Just do as I say and go fetch them for me."

He got them and brought them to his mother, and his mother prepared a dish such as his father liked. Rebekah then took the best clothes of her older son Esau, which were there in the house, and had her younger son Jacob put them on; and she covered his hands and the hairless part of his neck with the skins of the kids. Then she put in the hands of her son Jacob the dish and the bread that she had prepared.

He went to his father and said, "Father." And he said, "Yes, which of my sons are you?" Jacob said to his father, "I am Esau, your first-born; I have done as you told me. Pray sit up and eat of my game, that you may give me your innermost blessing." Isaac said to his son, "How did you succeed so quickly, my son?" And he said, "Because the Lord your God granted me good fortune." Isaac said to Jacob, "Come closer that I may feel you, my son—whether you are really my son Esau or not." So Jacob drew close to his father Isaac, who felt him and wondered. "The voice is the voice of Jacob, yet the hands are the hands of Esau." He did not recognize him, because his hands were hairy like those of his brother Esau; and so he blessed him (Genesis 27:1–23).

. . . Now Esau harbored a grudge against Jacob because of the blessing which his father had given him, and Esau said to himself, "Let but the mourning period of my father come, and I will kill my brother Jacob." When the words of her older son Esau were reported to Rebekah, she sent for her younger son Jacob and said to him, "Your brother Esau is consoling himself by planning to kill you. Now, my son, listen to me. Flee at once to Haran, to my brother Laban. Stay with him a while, until your brother's fury subsides—until your brother's anger against you subsides—and he forgets what you have done to him. Then I will fetch you from there. Let me not lose you both in one day!"

Rebekah said to Isaac, "I am disgusted with my life because of the Hittite women. If Jacob marries a Hittite woman like these, from among the native women, what good will life be to me?" So Isaac sent for Jacob and blessed him. He instructed him, saying, "You shall not take a wife from among the Canaanite women. Up, go to Paddan-aram, to the house of Bethuel, your mother's father, and take a wife there from among the daughters of Laban, your mother's brother (Genesis 27:40–28:2).

Rabbinic Midrashim

These midrashim tell us a lot about what the Rabbis thought of Rebekah. How do they compare to your interpretations? What question underlies the third midrash? Did this question trouble you? Are you satisfied with this answer? How well do you think the last midrash explains why Rebekah's death is not recorded in the TaNaKH?

The second and third midrashim seem to suggest that Rebekah usurped some of the prerogatives of her parents and her husband. Do you think these midrashim consider that praiseworthy? (Look again at the first and last midrashim.) Does this surprise you? Why do you think the Rabbis would reinforce this behavior?

AND SHE WENT DOWN TO THE FOUNTAIN, AND FILLED HER PITCHER (Genesis 24:16). All women went down and drew water from the well, whereas for her the water ascended as soon as it saw her.[2]

---

2. *Genesis Rabbah* 60:5, in *The Midrash*, ed. and trans. H. Freeman and Maurice Simon et al. (London: Soncino Press, 1951).

AND THEY CALLED REBEKAH, AND SAID UNTO HER: WILT THOU GO? (Genesis 24:58). R. Ḥanina, the son of R. Adda, said in R. Isaac's name: They hinted to her, WILT THOU [ACTUALLY] GO? AND SHE SAID: I WILL GO (ibid.): I go in spite of you, whether you wish or not.[3]

R. Levi taught that in the verse THE LORD SAID UNTO HER: TWO NATIONS ARE IN THY WOMB (Genesis 25:23), the words unto her imply that the Lord said to Rebekah: "I shall reveal a mystery to thee: From thee shall [Israel], the foremost of the nations, come forth." Hence [of Isaac to whom this mystery was not revealed] Scripture says NOW ISAAC LOVED ESAU (Genesis 25:28), whereas of Rebekah the verse goes on to say REBEKAH LOVED JACOB (Genesis 25:28), because she knew what the Holy One, blessed be He, had revealed to her.[4]

When Rebekah died, it was asked: Who will walk before her bier? Abraham is dead. Isaac stays at home because his eyes are dim, and Jacob has gone to Paddan-aram. Should wicked Esau walk before her bier, people will say, "A curse on the breast that gave suck to such a one." What did they do? They took her out for burial at night. For this reason, Scripture does not record her death.[5]

Dreams

by Zeise Wild Wolf

The biblical account of Rebekah and Jacob's lives together begins "This is the story of Isaac" (Genesis 25:19). Although, as we have seen, Rebekah is

---

3. *Genesis Rabbah* 60:12, in ibid.

4. "The Midrash on Psalms 9:7," in *The Midrash on Psalms*, trans. William G. Braude. (New Haven, CT: Yale University Press, 1959).

5. *Tanḥuma, Ki Tetze* 4; *Pesikta Rabbati* 12:4, in *The Book of Legends*, ed. Hayim Nahman Bialik and Yehoshua Hana Ravnitzky; trans. William G. Braude (New York: Schocken Books, 1992).

more active, we are told that this is Isaac's tale. Zeise Wild Wolf's "Dreams"
is the counterpoint. In effect, her telling could begin, "This is the story of
Rebekah." As you read, compare especially Rebekah's relationship with God in
this tale to the rabbinic understanding.

I had had dreams. Of a rich and handsome man who would ride into
town and take me away to live an adventurous, glamorous life. Dreams
born in a house of con-men and boring, snivelling little boys who stared
at me as if I already belonged to them. The old man described me well
when he said *almah*. I was ripe as the sweetest fruit, nearly bursting out
of my skin. And I was as innocent as any young girl who still giggles at
the thought of where babies came from. I look back on that girl with
fondness and chagrin. So eager. So naive.

Would I have done better with a different cousin? I torment myself
with the question, wishing but unable to answer, believably, NO. So
sometimes I imagine myself by the side of one of those boys from my
hometown. Now it is of them I dream.

All the girls in town were polite and sweet, and many of them were
beautiful. Any one of us would have answered the old servant the same
way, given the chance. Leaving with a stranger was a longshot, but to a
young girl a gamble can seem preferable to a sure, familiar life. Yet at first
I hesitated. The way the man told his story to my brother I was sure there
was something important he was not saying. My misgivings hardly
mattered, though. As soon as Lavan saw the gold on my arms that man
was guaranteed whatever he wanted. Any of the other girls would have
fared the same.

Broken man in the fields, in the distance, in the setting sun. The
sight of him tipped me from my camel in habitual deference and pity.
Who is that old man? I wondered, asked my guide as politely as I could.
I figured it was his own father, come to meet us and lead us in. That is
my lord, the kind man responded. I thought at first he must mean the
father, but he kept staring at me, as if waiting for something. It came to
me so slowly: less a thought than a sense. I veiled my face quickly, before
the hot tears spilled over to slide down my face. In the walk from my
camel to the broken man each step deadened a dream I'd held dear;

deadened dreaming itself; replaced a young girl's hoping for challenge and adventure with pity and a mother's love. Before I'd even reached him, before I'd even met him, Yitzkhak had become simply the first of my children, the oldest by several years. I ground bitter disappointment into dust beneath my feet, transformed step-by-step from a dreamy, wishful girl into a practical woman. The soil of my soul reconstituted itself from ash and defeat as my own feet delivered me to my destiny.

I tried to let the servant's retelling of our meeting cheer me, but despondency had settled on me like a heavy cloak. Luckily Yitzkhak did not try to speak to me. He did not touch me there, did not attempt to look beneath my veil. He simply led me toward the tent I learned later had been his mother's. I heard a sigh behind me, loud enough to reach my ears across the distance we had walked, and turned to see the servant sinking to his knees, the tears streaming down his face reflecting rainbows from the sun.

Yitzkhak drank from my breast. He suckled as though nursing and yet he was a man, not the baby to whom I had already resigned myself, and his aching longing enflamed me. He drank me as I arched beside him, sucked my breasts dry, covered my belly and back in fierce, hungry kisses that woke my skin and my soul from a lifelong sleep. He buried his face between my legs and his tongue filled and explored me, slowly danced against me until I shuddered and moaned. He raised his face to mine and we kissed. We moved together. He entered inside me and I pulled him closer, until he bound his soul to mine, until he withdrew his heart and soul from his mother and father and placed them in me. We stayed together that night and he touched me all the ways I had so long ago imagined, giggling, someone might. In the language my body spoke Yitzkhak was comforted. But I? I dreaded for the night to end. I knew as if I had been told that it was only there, under cover of dark, that I had an equal. As though I had lived already all that was to come, day was as I had known it would be just from seeing him in the distance, just from lying beside him as night gave way to morning. In the world outside our tent Yitzkhak was practically ineffectual. I ran the camp, our home, our life.

This is the sound of a heart breaking: my footsteps grinding sand to dust. In my dreams I walk, veiled, toward my future. Sometimes I turn to the left or right before he reaches me, before he claims me with his touch.

Sometimes I wave from a distance, then run back to my camel and try to ride away, to flee. Whichever I choose I am lying beside Yitzkhak when I wake, his breath on my neck, my face. I gather myself before he opens his eyes, try to cover myself with an expression he cannot penetrate. It is no use. My eyes will not be still. My heart bleeds out of their sockets and oozes to the ground. With just a glance he reads my regret as if I spoke. He turns aside, shoulders hunched forward as if he will lean to the earth and gather my heart with his trembling hands. Yitzkhak, I say softly, and touch him gently. He turns his body toward me, but keeps his face averted. I'm sorry, he says, so quietly that I am not sure he has spoken until the breath catches in his throat.

We lived like this. In the nights we exacted our relief in the world beyond words. We buried our disappointments and fed our insatiable hungers with our mouths, with our hands. I raged at him with my caresses, I beat at him as I drew him into me, pushed him out again. With kisses he begged me, buried his face between my labia and talked to me of all he would have been. By our sighs and moans we fought and forgave. But with our screams and our laughter mingled the dread of morning.

Perhaps it was because I was so impatient with him that he finally told me his story, though he began it in the safety of evening, speaking into the quiet, dark tent. He spoke as if he had never formed words before, each thought, each phrase, rusty and raw. I had heard rumors of course, but I thought them preposterous and his story was anyway worse than the rumors I had heard, worse than I would have thought I could believe. A man whose own father tied him to wood and laid him out for sacrifice, whose own father raised a knife to plunder his flesh, whose eyes flashed in the sun as his boy lay helpless beneath him. A man whose father was so eager to please his god that his name had to be called twice to stay his hand.

I had wanted to hate this man, my husband, for his weakness and passivity; I had tried to pity him, this man who broke every one of my dreams by being not strong and courageous but timid and quiet and afraid, this man who turned gold bracelets on my wrists to chains. I tried to imagine: what if my own father had tried to kill me. I would have fought. I would have yelled. I would have taken the knife and killed him instead. But my own father would not have tried to kill me; it occurred to me that perhaps my fight came from knowing that. I tried to imagine what might cause a strong, grown man to lie still beneath a knife blade in the hand of an old, weak one. I thought if I could imagine I could forgive Yitzkhak his quiet ways, his nightmares, his vulnerability. I could not imagine. Yet I forgave him completely.

I began to sense why I had been chosen to be his wife. I was strong enough to do what had to be done. I didn't like the sound of this god, and yet I felt I understood, that I knew what was required. It was suddenly necessary to have children.

Ask God, I urged Yitzkhak. You're owed something for all your suffering. Yitzkhak agreed, but it took him weeks to do it. You're owed at least this, I told him again, and finally he spoke. We lay together and I conceived, and my belly swelled and grew. But a battle brewed within me. Mystified, I spoke to this god myself; thus I learned my children's future before they breathed a single breath of this world's air.

From the beginning I preferred Ya'akov, the cunning boy who held onto his brother's heel to ease his passage into the world. Yitzkhak preferred the hairy red one, Aysav. It seemed better to have favorites with twins. One day my boy told me how he had tricked for himself his brother's birthright. I was shocked and offended. Thus you treat your own brother? I asked. Then I remembered the words God spoke before their birth: "The greater will serve the younger." I wondered at my memory. Did this god approve trickery? I remembered the words of my own mother and brother to the old man who would take me from their home. "This thing comes from God," they had said. "It is not possible for us to speak to you good or bad." I had always thought they agreed with the servant's request. It occurred to me that perhaps they merely stood as I stood before my own child, saying nothing, silenced on the threshold of speech. I spoke no praise to my child, but neither did I rebuke him further, and he swaggered away, grinning wide.

The next morning I got up early and slipped from the tent without waking Yizkhak. I felt strange, disturbed, as if I did not know who I was. When a girl, ripe and virgin and ready to be swept away by a strange man for a life of excitement, I imagined myself pure and good. I had strong morals and deep convictions. I was kind to strangers, generous to the needy. I believed in fairness. I despised my brother Lavan for his cunning ways and resented my mother for tolerating them. But suddenly nothing seemed so clear. This god I spoke with, who revealed to me my babies' future before they were born, seemed to prefer my son's cunning to the generosity I had tried to teach him to exhibit. My earlier morality seemed like a kind of arrogance, so that I could remember my past way but not desire it, despite my efforts to do so. I could see what was wrong with Ya'akov's behavior but I could not condemn it. Yet who was I, if not the total of my convictions? I felt terribly lonely, so lost. The murmurings of the dawn camp melded with the wind. Somewhere between our tent and the edge of camp I realized that I was Avraham's kin. A wrenching feeling in my stomach taught me, long before I was required, that one day I too would betray Yitzkhak to fulfill this god's wishes. I cried out loud at the thought, which cut me then as Avraham's knife would have cut my husband long ago, given the chance. I thought of how Yitzkhak's face would crumple as he realized I had sided with God against him. I closed my eyes but his face rose up before me in the darkness. I willed Yitzkhak to know how deeply I had come to love him, though I had hardly known it myself until that morning. Then I wiped away my tears, and prepared to live the life I'd been given to lead. And when, so much later, I saw my work before me, I tried to swallow my sorrow and do what I was called upon to do.

Yitzkhak, I felt sure, knew he was being deceived. Though there was much he chose not to see, perhaps could not see, he certainly knew one son from the other, and I saw pass across his face, as he pressed his hands to the skins covering his youngest boy's arms comprehension, sadness such as I have never witnessed and would not have guessed could be survived, resignation. I watched as he gave up, gave in finally to his God, to me, to his own son; to his father, to a world he could not understand, to a whole way of living against which he felt defenseless. I watched Ya'akov, who would have minded getting caught but enjoyed the deception itself, with a horror that severed the bond between us that I had nurtured since his birth. What had I created in this boy? But it was too late for that and I cursed God, who seemed to pat my back and soothe me, to remind me of all I had once understood, one early morning, so terribly long ago.

Lest Aysav too bring sin upon his own head I sent Ya'akov away. I did not need to hesitate before choosing his destination: a boy willing to steal from his brother and deceive his father would get on well enough with

Lavan. For a few days, I said, but I knew I would never see my youngest child again. It seemed I should have minded more than I did.

That night Yitzkhak did not kiss me, though he lay beside me. I did not try to speak. I could not think of any words to build a bridge over the chasm he faced. Yitzkhak had hoped in me, had loved me as a prayer that had inevitably failed to be answered. I had shielded him both too late and too soon to protect him from the deep suffering his God required. I knew this, as I knew the terrible loneliness that is the one true fact of being. Yet I stretched my arm across the space between us and lay my hand over his heart. He grabbed it fiercely, as if to fling it from his chest. He turned toward me and pulled me close to him. And we cried together as the night gave way to morning, and in each other found comfort.

5

Leah and Rachel

Leah and Rachel in the Bible

The Rachel and Leah narratives are complex, full of deceit and betrayal across a wide range of relationships. As you read, look especially for clues to the relationship between the two sisters. How did Laban, their father, and Jacob, the husband they shared, affect their relationship?

Do you think it was possible for Jacob to have been so easily fooled into marrying the "wrong" sister? Why didn't Jacob ever come to love Leah? Pay particular attention to the names that Leah gives to her sons. To whom are they directed? What do they reveal about Leah? What about the names Rachel gives to Bilhah's sons?

What do you think about Jacob's response to Rachel's plea for children? Why might Rachel have stolen her father's idols? Was her death punishment for the theft?

Jacob resumed his journey and came to the land of the Easterners. There before his eyes was a well in the open. Three flocks of sheep were lying there beside it, for the flocks were watered from that well. The stone on the mouth of the well was large. When all the flocks were gathered there, the stone would be rolled from the mouth of the well and the sheep watered; then the stone would be put back in its place on the mouth of the well.

Jacob said to them, "My friends, where are you from?" And they said, "We are from Haran." He said to them, "Do you know Laban the son of Nahor?" And they said, "Yes, we do." He continued, "Is he well?" They answered, "Yes, he is; and there is his daughter Rachel, coming with the flock." He said, "It is still broad daylight, too early to round up the animals; water the flock and take them to pasture." But they said, "We cannot, until all the flocks are rounded up; then the stone is rolled off the mouth of the well and we water the sheep."

While he was still speaking with them, Rachel came with her father's flock; for she was a shepherdess. And when Jacob saw Rachel, the daughter of his uncle Laban, and the flock of his uncle Laban, Jacob went up and rolled the stone off the mouth of the well, and watered the flock of his uncle Laban. Then Jacob kissed Rachel, and broke into tears. Jacob told Rachel that he was her father's kinsman, that he was Rebekah's son; and she ran and told her father. On hearing the news of his sister's son Jacob, Laban ran to greet him; he embraced him and kissed him, and took him into his house. He told Laban all that had happened, and Laban said to him, "You are truly my bone and flesh."

When he had stayed with him a month's time, Laban said to Jacob, "Just because you are a kinsman, should you serve me for nothing? Tell me, what shall your wages be?" Now Laban had two daughters; the name of the older one was Leah, and the name of the younger was Rachel. Leah had weak eyes; Rachel was shapely and beautiful. Jacob loved Rachel; so he answered, "I will serve you seven years for your younger daughter Rachel." Laban said, "Better that I give her to you than that I should give her to an outsider. Stay with me." So Jacob served seven years for Rachel and they seemed to him but a few days because of his love for her.

Then Jacob said to Laban, "Give me my wife, for my time is fulfilled, that I may cohabit with her." And Laban gathered all the people of the place and made a feast. When evening came, he took his daughter Leah and brought her to him; and he cohabitated with her.—Laban had given his maidservant Zilpah to his daughter Leah as her maid.—When morning came, there was Leah! So he said to Laban, "What is this you have done to me? I was in your service for Rachel! Why did you deceive me?" Laban said, "It is not the practice in our place to marry off the younger before the older. Wait until the bridal week of this one is over and we will give you that one too, provided you serve me another seven years." Jacob did so; he waited out the bridal week of the one, and then he gave him his daughter Rachel as wife.—Laban had given his maidservant Bilhah to his daughter Rachel as her maid.—And Jacob cohabitated with Rachel also; indeed, he loved Rachel more than Leah. And he served him another seven years.

The Lord saw that Leah was unloved and he opened her womb; but Rachel was barren. Leah conceived and bore a son, and named him Reuben; for she declared, "It means: 'The Lord has seen my affliction'; it also means: 'Now my husband will love me.'" She conceived again and bore a son, and declared, "This is because the Lord heard that I was unloved and has given me this one also"; so she named him Simeon. Again she conceived and bore a son and declared, "This time my husband will become attached to me, for I have borne him three sons." Therefore he was named Levi. She conceived again and bore a son, and declared, "This time I will praise the Lord." Therefore she named him Judah. Then she stopped bearing.

When Rachel saw that she had borne Jacob no children, she became envious of her sister; and Rachel said to Jacob, "Give me children, or I shall die." Jacob was incensed at Rachel, and said, "Can I take the place of God, who has denied you fruit of the womb?" She said, "Here is my maid Bilhah. Consort with her, that she may bear on my knees and that through her I too may have children." So she gave him her maid Bilhah as a concubine, and Jacob cohabitated with her. Bilhah conceived and bore Jacob a son. And Rachel said, "God has vindicated me; indeed, He has heeded my plea and given me a son." Therefore she named him Dan. Rachel's maid Bilhah conceived again and bore Jacob a second son. And Rachel said, "A fateful contest I waged with my sister; yes, and I have prevailed." So she named him Naphtali.

When Leah saw that she had stopped bearing, she took her maid Zilpah and gave her to Jacob as concubine. And when Leah's maid Zilpah bore Jacob a son, Leah said, "What luck!" So she named him Gad. When Leah's maid Zilpah bore Jacob a second son, Leah declared, "What fortune!" meaning, "Women will deem me fortunate." So she named him Asher.

Once, at the time of the wheat harvest, Reuben came upon some mandrakes in the field and brought them to his mother Leah. Rachel said to Leah, "Please give me some of your son's mandrakes." But she said to her, "Was it not enough for you to take away my husband, that you would also take my son's mandrakes?" Rachel replied, "I promise, he shall lie with you tonight, in return for your son's mandrakes." When Jacob came home from the field in the evening, Leah went out to meet him and said, "You are to sleep with me, for I have hired you with my son's mandrakes." And he lay with her that night. God heeded Leah, and she conceived and bore him a fifth son. And Leah said, "God has given me my reward for having given my maid to my husband." So she named him Issachar. When Leah conceived again and bore Jacob a sixth son, Leah said, "God has given me a choice gift; this time my husband will exalt me, for I have borne him six sons." So she named him Zebulun. Last, she bore him a daughter, and named her Dinah.

Now God remembered Rachel; God heeded her and opened her womb. She conceived and bore a son, and said, "God has taken away my disgrace." So she named him Joseph, which is to say, "May the Lord add another son for me" (Genesis 29:1–30:24).

. . . Now he heard the things that Laban's sons were saying: "Jacob has taken all that was our father's, and from that which was our father's he has built up all this wealth." Jacob also saw that Laban's manner toward him was not as it had been in the past. Then the Lord said to Jacob, "Return to the land of your fathers where you were born, and I will be with you." Jacob had Rachel and Leah called to the field, where his flock was, and said to them, "I see that your father's manner toward me is not as it has been in the past. But the God of my father has been with me. As you know, I have served your father with all my might; but your father has cheated me, changing my wages time and again. God, however, would not let him do me harm. If he said thus, 'The speckled shall be your wages,' then all the flocks would drop speckled young; and if he said thus, 'The streaked shall be your wages,' then all the flocks would drop streaked young. God has taken away your father's livestock and given it to me (Genesis 31:1–9).

. . . Then Rachel and Leah answered him saying, "Have we still a share in the inheritance of our father's house? Surely, he regards us as outsiders, now that he has sold us and has used up our purchase price. Truly, all the wealth that God has taken away from our father belongs to us and to our children. Now then, do just as God has told you."

Thereupon Jacob put his children and wives on camels; and he drove off all his livestock and all the wealth that he had amassed, the livestock in his possession that he had acquired in Paddan-aram, to go to his father Isaac in the land of Canaan.

Meanwhile, Laban had gone to shear his sheep, and Rachel stole her father's household idols. Jacob kept Laban the Aramean in the dark, not telling him that he was fleeing, and fled with all that he had. Soon he was across the Euphrates and heading toward the hill country of Gilead.

On the third day, Laban was told that Jacob had fled. So he took his kinsmen with him and pursued him a distance of seven days, catching up with him in the hill country of Gilead. But God appeared to Laban the Aramean in a dream by night and said to him, "Beware of attempting anything with Jacob, good or bad."

Laban overtook Jacob. Jacob had pitched his tent on the Height, and Laban with his kinsmen encamped in the hill country of Gilead. And Laban said to Jacob, "What did you mean by keeping me in the dark and carrying off my daughters like captives of the sword? Why did you flee in secrecy and mislead me and not tell me? I would have sent you off with festive music, with timbrel and lyre. You did not even let me kiss my sons and daughters good-by! It was a foolish thing for you to do. I have it in my power to do you harm; but the God of your father said to me last night, 'Beware of attempting anything with Jacob, good or bad.' Very well, you had to leave because you were longing for your father's house; but why did you steal my gods?"

Jacob answered Laban, saying, "I was afraid because I thought you would take your daughters from me by force. But anyone with whom you find your gods shall not remain alive! In the presence of our kinsmen, point out what I have of yours and take it." Jacob, of course, did not know that Rachel had stolen them.

So Laban went into Jacob's tent and Leah's tent and the tents of the two maidservants; but he did not find them. Leaving Leah's tent, he entered Rachel's tent. Rachel, meanwhile, had taken the idols and placed them in the camel cushion and sat on them; and Laban rummaged through the tent without finding them. For she said to her father, "Let not my lord take it amiss that I cannot rise before you, for the period of women is upon me." Thus he searched, but could not find the household idols (Genesis 31:14–35).

{Jacob and Laban make peace between themselves, and Jacob and his family continue their journey back to the land of his birth.}

. . . They set out from Bethel; but when they were still some distance short of Ephrath, Rachel was in childbirth, and she had hard labor. When her labor was at its hardest, the midwife said to her, "Have no fear, for it is another boy for you." But as she breathed her last—for she was dying—she named him Ben-oni; but his father called him Benjamin. Thus Rachel died. She was buried on the road to Ephrath— now Bethlehem. Over her grave, Jacob set up a pillar; it is the pillar at Rachel's grave to this day (Genesis 35:16–20).

Rabbinic Midrashim

Both Leah and Rachel appear as assertive women in these rabbinic midrashim. But consider: what is the result of Leah's response to Jacob's insults? How does Jacob respond to Rachel's admonishments? God hears Rachel's pleas in the last midrash, and responds, but what kind of behavior is she citing in her argument?

All night, she pretended to be Rachel. When he arose in the morning [according to Genesis 29:25], THERE WAS LEAH. He said to her: Daughter of a swindler, why did you trick me? She said to him: [What about] you! Why did you trick your father? When he said to you: Is this my son Esau, you said to him [in Genesis 27:19]: I AM ESAU YOUR FIRST-BORN. Now you are saying: Why have you tricked me? And did your father not say [to Esau] [in Genesis 27:35]: YOUR BROTHER CAME WITH DECEIT? So, because of these things with which she scolded him, he began to hate her. The Holy One said: There is no cure for this but sons. Then her husband will desire her. Thus [in

Genesis 29:31]: WHEN THE LORD SAW THAT LEAH WAS HATED, HE OPENED HER WOMB.[1]

Rachel said to Jacob [in Genesis 30:1–2]: GIVE ME CHILDREN, OR ELSE I SHALL DIE. THEN JACOB'S ANGER WAS KINDLED AGAINST RACHEL. . . . She said to him: Did your father, Isaac, do this to your mother, Rebekah? Did not the two of them stand and pray for each other? It is so stated [in Genesis 25:21] THEN ISAAC ENTREATED THE LORD ON BEHALF OF HIS WIFE. You should also pray unto the Lord for me! And did not your grandfather Abraham do this for Sarah? He said to her: Sarah brought a rival wife into her house. She said to him [in Genesis 30:3]: If so, HERE IS MY MAID BILHAH; GO IN TO HER.[2]

{God and the ministering Angels, led by Jeremiah, go out to see the remains of the Temple in Jerusalem, destroyed as a punishment by God for Israel's sins. God weeps and tells Jeremiah to get Abraham, Isaac, Jacob, and Moses from their tombs to mourn with Him. All four of them beg God to remember Israel because of their deeds.}

At that moment, the matriarch Rachel broke forth into speech before the Holy One, blessed be He, and said, "Sovereign of the Universe, it is revealed before Thee that Thy servant Jacob loved me exceedingly and toiled for my father on my behalf seven years. When those seven years were completed and the time arrived for my marriage with my husband, my father planned to substitute another for me to wed my husband for the sake of my sister. It was very hard for me because the plot was known to me and I disclosed it to my husband; and I gave him a sign whereby he could distinguish between me and my sister, so that my father should not be able to make the substitution. After that I relented, suppressed my desire, and had pity upon my sister that she should not be exposed to shame. In the evening they substituted my sister for me with my husband, and I delivered over to my sister all the signs which I had arranged with my husband so he should think that she was Rachel. More

---

1. *Midrash Tanhuma* 7:11, in *Midrash Tanhuman*, trans. John T. Townsend (Hoboken, NJ: Ktav Publishing House, 1989).

2. *Midrash Tanhuma* 7:19, in ibid.

than that, I went beneath the bed upon which he lay with my sister; and when he spoke to her she remained silent, and I made all the replies in order that he should not recognize my sister's voice. I did her a kindness, was not jealous of her, and did not expose her to shame. And if I, a creature of flesh and blood, formed of dust and ashes, was not envious of my rival and did not expose her to shame and contempt, why shouldst Thou, a King Who liveth eternally and art merciful, be jealous of idolatry in which there is no reality, and exile my children and let them be slain by the sword, and their enemies have done with them as they wished!"

Forthwith, the mercy of the Holy One, blessed be He, was stirred, and He said, "For thy sake Rachel, I will restore Israel to their place." And so it is written, THUS SAITH THE LORD: A VOICE IS HEARD IN RAMAH, LAMENTATIONS AND BITTER WEEPING, RACHEL WEEPING FOR HER CHILDREN; SHE REFUSETH TO BE COM-FORTED FOR HER CHILDREN, BECAUSE THEY ARE NOT [Jeremiah 31:15]. This is followed by, THUS SAITH THE LORD: REFRAIN THY VOICE FROM WEEPING, AND THINE EYES FROM TEARS; FOR THY WORK SHALL BE REWARDED. . . . AND THERE IS HOPE FOR THY FUTURE, SAITH THE LORD; AND THY CHILDREN SHALL RETURN TO THEIR OWN BORDER (ibid., 16–17).[3]

Leah

by Naomi Hyman

Even in most contemporary, egalitarian prayers, only Rachel and Leah are included among the Matriarchs and the younger, beloved wife always precedes the older, flawed sister in the recitation of their names. How did life look through Leah's eyes? How credible is the idea, explored here and above, that Rachel participated in the deception of Jacob in order to protect her sister?

---

3. *Lamentations Rabbah*, Proem 24, in *The Midrash*, ed. and trans. H. Freedman and Maurice Simon et al. (London: Soncino Press, 1951).

~◦~

As long as I can remember, I have been called Leah of the weak eyes. Never Leah of the lush hair or even quiet Leah. All my life—except when the babies started coming—I've been defined by my failures.

My father, Laban, never tried to hide his disappointment. It was bad enough that his firstborn was a girl. Then it became clear to everyone—as I stumbled over things others stepped around or got lost playing in the yard—that I couldn't see. I was not just a girl; I was a defective one. It was as if my flaws somehow diminished him. Perhaps they did.

It was clear enough that I couldn't do more than the simplest tasks. I couldn't tend the herds (how would I ever see a stray?) or even draw the water (I couldn't find my way back home). I would be a burden to my father all the days of his life. A burden and an embarrassment. A sign of his failure. He hated even to see me.

On a good day, if I stayed out of his way, there was the safety of invisibility. On a bad day, he sought me out, as if he could beat away his failures by eradicating the symbol of them. I learned to find the shadows by their coolness and I hid there.

My sister, Rachel, was my lifeline to the sun. She was my guide and my protector. She would take my hand and lead me into the fields behind our house. She found beautiful things—a flower, a shiny pebble, a soft and tickly feather—and she brought them close so I could see them. Sometimes, we'd sit huddled together on the stone wall, watching the sun go down. Rachel would describe the changing colors and the way the stars appeared in the suddenly black sky. I taught her to feel the way the air around us cooled and to hear the new music as the day creatures yielded the world to the ones who lived in the dark. At night, we would snuggle together in our bed, and even though I was bigger, she made me feel safe.

As we got older, Rachel was drawn more and more into the world of women. She had many chores now, but she loved watering the sheep best of all. Each day she met the other young women at the well where they giggled and gossiped. Late at night, lying in our bed, she whispered the secrets she had learned. Soon, the news was of marriages, and I tried not to show my fear and jealousy.

I'd known for a long time that I would never marry, but the ache of that knowledge never went away. I loved the way my little brothers and sisters felt in my arms and the warm, milky way they smelled. I wanted so much to feel my own children sleeping in my arms, to shelter and protect them. I wondered what it would be like to have a man love me, to feel safe in his bed the way I did with Rachel. Instead, I knew, I would spend my years caring for my father as best I could, always disappointing him, always shaming him. And Rachel would be gone, and with her all comfort.

One evening, Rachel returned from the well so bright with happiness that even I could see her glow. But there was a guest for dinner, and it was hours before we climbed, exhausted, into bed. In breathless whispers, she told me all about Jacob, our guest, about the way her heart beat when she saw him, how she couldn't look at him without blushing. She was going to marry him, she said. I tried, oh I tried only to show happiness for her, but I felt my body pull away from her. I loved her so much, and I did want her to be happy, but how would I bear the life ahead of me?

A month later, Laban announced that he had given Jacob permission to marry Rachel. In return, Jacob would work for him for seven years. I listened to Rachel's breath catch, and then sink into a moan as she realized what this meant, but I felt only relief. There would be a reprieve! A seven-year reprieve! It seemed a lifetime.

Life resumed its old patterns, but some nights Rachel would creep into our bed long after I had fallen asleep. The days passed so slowly for her, as she waited for the day when she would be joined with her love. For me, they flew from my hands like the butterflies Rachel caught for me when we were children laughing in the field.

In the seventh year, I felt heaviness creep into my limbs. I stayed more and more in the shadows, hiding now from my radiant sister. "Leah," she would call, "Leah, come, let us watch the sun set together." But I would sink deeper into the dark.

One day, she found me in my quiet place, and she sank down onto her heels beside me. Her glance held so much love and hope. Hot tears leaked from my eyes. I didn't want to curse her happiness. I didn't want her to know the bitterness that I felt. Rachel spoke not a word, but settled down beside me. After a while, she wrapped her arm around me, and laid her head on my shoulder. "Tell me," she said. Again, quietly, "Tell me."

I just turned my head and looked at her sweet face, close enough for me to see the brown wells of her eyes, the sharp lines of her cheekbones, the downy hair at her temples. We sat a long time together, not speaking.

That night, for the first time in many weeks, she came to bed early. "I've spoken with father," she said. "It is you who will marry Jacob." I started to rise, to speak, but she laid a finger on my lips, silencing me. "You know how greedy our father is. I told him that I had a plan that would double my bride price. 'You know how much Jacob loves me,' I told him. 'If he would work seven years for me, why not fourteen? Let us secretly marry him to Leah. You will be rid of her, and surely Jacob will work another seven years for me.' You should have seen his eyes light up, the old fool! Now it is done. Jacob will be angry at the deception, but he is a good man and he will come to love you like I do. Soon enough, I will join you and we will be together again like we were as children." I tried to protest, but she would have none of it. "This way I can protect you, and keep you near to me."

Rachel taught me signs so that Jacob would not know of the deception until it was morning and our marriage consummated. Suddenly, it seemed, I stood veiled beneath the *chuppah*, astonished that such a thing should be. That night, I became Jacob's wife.

In the morning I woke to his angry cries. A week later, he married Rachel.

Jacob never did come to love me. Like my father, he could barely stand the sight of me, but that did not keep him from my bed. When he was done with me, he pushed away absentmindedly, as if leaving the table. He rarely spoke a word to me.

In time, I conceived. I looked forward to the birth of the child. Perhaps, if it was a son, Jacob might come to love me. But even if he did not, Rachel would surely help me raise the child and we would be a family. When the birthing time arrived, Rachel did not come. I longed for her touch during those hours of pain, but I was too exhausted by the labor to think about it.

Instead of bringing us closer, my child seemed to be a wedge between us. Gone was her carefree, confident way with Jacob. She hovered over him and flirted with him. She bought pots of paint for her face, and prepared for hours for his visits. I had become her rival, the wife of her husband and the mother of her children.

I bore more children, she none. She would not—could not—accept my comfort. I hated her for hating me. We began our bitter war, using our maidservants against one another. I imagined Jacob chuckling at our jealous games and relishing his small harem.

Finally, oh thank God, finally, Rachel conceived and bore Joseph. Gently, slowly, we began to speak again. Then she conceived again and the wall between us crumbled. We giggled together and shared secrets with each other, laughing even at Jacob. When the birthing time came, I was with her.

But Rachel had hard labor. She grew weak and pale as she struggled; her grip on my hand faded. They tore the child from her as she cried out and died.

Rachel, my sister, my rival, my friend, when you named him Ben-Oni, child of your pain, I thought no, it should be child of *our* pain. For you lie beneath the earth at the side of the road, and Jacob is withered without you. And I, I am an old woman now, caring for him as best I can, and always disappointing.

6

DINAH

Dinah in the Bible

Dinah is the daughter of Leah and sister to the twelve sons of Jacob (who will give their names to the twelve tribes of Israel). Shimon and Levi, who figure prominently in this story, were her full brothers, sons of Leah and Jacob. As you read through this account, look for Dinah's actions and words. What do you make of her silence? Consider the way in which the text characterizes the act of rape. On whom is the injury inflicted? Compare Jacob's reaction to that of Dinah's brothers. Do you think that the punishment is appropriate?

Now Dinah, the daughter whom Leah had borne to Jacob, went out to visit the daughters of the land. Shechem son of Hamor the Hivite, chief of the country, saw her, and took her and lay with her by force. Being strongly drawn to Dinah daughter of Jacob, and in love with the maiden, he spoke to the maiden tenderly. So Shechem said to his father Hamor, "Get me this girl as a wife."

Jacob heard that he had defiled his daughter Dinah; but since his sons were in the field with his cattle, Jacob kept silent until they came home. Then Shechem's father Hamor came out to Jacob to speak to him.

65

Meanwhile, Jacob's sons, having heard the news, came in from the field. The men were distressed and very angry, because he had committed an outrage in Israel by lying with Jacob's daughter—a thing not to be done.

And Hamor spoke with them, saying, "My son Shechem longs for your daughter. Please give her to him in marriage. Intermarry with us: give your daughter to us, and take our daughters for yourselves: You will dwell among us, and the land will be open before you; settle, move about, and acquire holdings in it." Then Shechem said to her father and brothers, "Do me this favor, and I will pay whatever you tell me. Ask of me a bride-price ever so high, as well as gifts, and I will pay what you tell me; only give me the maiden for a wife."

Jacob's sons answered Shechem and his father Hamor—speaking with guile because he had defiled their sister Dinah—and said to them, "We cannot do this thing, to give our sister to a man who is uncircumcised, for that is a disgrace among us. Only on this condition will we agree with you; that you will become like us in that every male among you is circumcised. Then we will give our daughters to you and take your daughters to ourselves; and we will dwell among you and become as one kindred. But if you will not listen to us and become circumcised, we will take our daughter and go."

Their words pleased Hamor and Hamor's son Shechem. And the youth lost no time in doing the thing, for he wanted Jacob's daughter. Now he was the most respected in his father's house. So Hamor and his son Shechem went to the public place of their town and spoke to their fellow townsmen, saying, "These people are our friends; let them settle in the land and move about in it, for the land is large enough for them; we will take their daughters to ourselves as wives and give our daughters to them. But only on this condition will the men agree with us to dwell among us and be as one kindred: that all our males become circumcised as they are circumcised. Their cattle and substance and all their beasts will be ours, if we only agree to their terms, so that they will settle among us." All who went out of the gate of his town heeded Hamor and his son Shechem, and all males, all those who went out of the gate of his town, were circumcised.

On the third day, when they were in pain, Simeon and Levi, two of Jacob's sons, brothers of Dinah, took each his sword, came upon the city unmolested, and slew all the males. They put Hamor and his son Shechem to the sword, took Dinah out of Shechem's house, and went away. The other sons of Jacob came upon the slain and plundered the town, because their sister had been defiled. They seized their flocks and herds and asses, all that was inside the town and outside; all their wealth, all their children, and their wives, all that was in the houses, they took as captives and booty.

Jacob said to Simeon and Levi, "You have brought trouble on me, making me odious among the inhabitants of the land, the Canaanites and the Perizzites; my men are few in number, so that if they unite against me and attack me, I and my house will be destroyed." But they answered, "Should our sister be treated like a whore?" (Genesis 34:1–31).

Rabbinic Midrashim

Although the biblical text condemns rape in general and Shechem's actions in particular, the midrashim presented here also blame Dinah, the victim. Do these interpretations sound familiar to you? How might these midrashim have differed had women been part of the process?

It is interesting to note that Leah is also condemned by the rabbinic tradition for going out, even though she was going to meet her husband (Genesis 30:16). Some (i.e., Midrash Tanhuma 8:14) see in this account the origin of the proverb "Like mother, like daughter" (Ezekiel 16:44).

~❦~

While her father and brothers were sitting in the House of Study, SHE WENT OUT TO SEE THE DAUGHTERS OF THE LAND [Genesis 34:1]. She brought upon herself her violation by Shechem the son of Hamor the Hivite, who is called a serpent, and he bit her; as it is written, AND SHECHEM THE SON OF HAMOR THE HIVITE, THE PRINCE OF THE LAND, SAW HER, AND HE TOOK HER, ETC. (ibid., 34:2). HE TOOK HER—he spoke seductively to her, as the word is used in TAKE WITH YOUR WORDS (Hosea 14:3); AND LAY WITH HER—in natural intercourse; AND HUMBLED HER—in unnatural intercourse.[1]

---

1. *Ecclesiastes Rabbah* 10:8, in *The Midrash*, ed. and trans. H. Freedman and Maurice Simon et al. (London: Soncino Press, 1951). The text connects Hivite with the similar-sounding Aramaic word for 'serpent'.

THEN GOD BLESSED THEM, AND GOD SAID TO THEM: [BE FRUITFUL AND MULTIPLY, FILL THE EARTH] AND SUBDUE HER (Genesis 1:28). The man subdues the woman, and the woman does not subdue the man. But, if she walks about a lot and goes out into the marketplace, she finally comes to a state of corruption, to a state of harlotry. And so you find in the case of Jacob's daughter Dinah. All the time that she was sitting at home, she was not corrupted by transgression; but, as soon as she went out into the marketplace, she caused herself to come to the point of corruption.[2]

R. Judah b. Simon commenced: BOAST NOT THYSELF OF TOMORROW (Proverbs 27:1), yet you [Jacob] have said, SO SHALL MY RIGHTEOUSNESS WITNESS FOR ME TOMORROW [Genesis 30:33]! Tomorrow your daughter will go out and be violated. Thus it is written, AND DINAH THE DAUGHTER OF LEAH WENT OUT [Genesis 34:1].[3]

AND TOOK DINAH OUT OF SHECHEM'S HOUSE AND WENT FORTH {Genesis 34:26}. R. Judah said: They dragged her out and departed. R. Ḥunia observed: When a woman is intimate with an uncircumcised person, she finds it hard to tear herself away. R. Huna [also] said: She pleaded, "AND I, WHITHER SHALL I CARRY MY SHAME?" [2 Samuel 13:13].[4]

A Daughter in Israel Is Raped

by Naomi Graetz

Naomi Graetz gives voice to the silent Dinah in "A Daughter in Israel Is Raped." What issues does she raise that the midrashim did not consider? Do you agree with Dinah's reaction to her brothers' plan for revenge?

---

2. *Midrash Tanhuma* 8:12, in *Midrash Tanhuman*, trans. John T. Townsend (Hoboken, NJ: Ktav Publishing House, 1989).
3. *Genesis Rabbah* 80:4, in *The Midrash*, ed. and trans. H. Freedman and Maurice Simon et al. (London: Soncino Press, 1951).
4. *Genesis Rabbah* 80:11, in ibid.

~❦~

They are tearing me apart. Will it never end?

When I was much younger than I am today, I was raped. I remember how the pain seared through me and how afterwards, I couldn't stop shaking.

For months I was in a constant state of fear that it might happen to me again and that was when I stopped going out to the fields for they were no longer safe. I still carefully check to see that no one suspicious is lurking around when I go out to tend animals.

I wasn't always a coward. Once I was known as princess Dinah, daughter of Jacob's first wife, Leah. I had six adoring brothers who took me with them wherever they went and who confided their secrets to me. I had many friends who visited me and I in turn visited with them.

One morning I crossed the mountain pass to spend a few days with the girls in the neighboring village. I had plenty of time to pick some wild flowers, which I did. Shechem was out hunting and saw me alone. I had seen him before. I knew who he was. He greeted me. I wasn't afraid. Then suddenly he threw me down and abused me. Against my will, he forced me to lie with him. I screamed and screamed, "Help me!" "Save me!" "Stop!" "Don't do it!" "Leave me alone!" But no one heard. Afterwards he dragged me to his father's home, alleging that he loved me and wanted to marry me.

Why did he single me out? I didn't like him. I didn't lead him on. I was just there. And he thought I wanted him after what he did.

My mother, Leah, came to the town of Shechem to persuade me I had no choice but to marry him after he had carried me off. She tried to console me by saying, "It's not the end of the world. He wants to marry you. His father is the chieftain of his clan. You'll be comfortable here. You will learn to live with him and love him."

She went on and on. I felt only the throbbing pain inside me and a feeling of shame. "Take what you can get. No one else will want you now! Be happy he still loves you," she said.

How could my mother think of marriage? Didn't she remember her own loveless marriage?

I yearned for my old way of life. But my innocence had been stolen. The old me no longer existed and it took an eternity to make peace with the new me. I had become a soiled object, someone to be pitied, to be quickly disposed of in marriage. I was someone who had to be revenged, who was ruined and undesirable, hating my body for its remembrance of what was.

My father, Jacob, was furious. He blamed me. He railed at me, "Why were you out in the fields by yourself?" He kept probing me, "Are you sure you didn't lead him on?" He insulted me by insinuating that I was guilty. But when my brothers discussed revenge he remained conspicuously silent.

Why did father blame me? I was as innocent as the virgin land we had settled. He had never warned me about the dangers awaiting young girls. How could he think I would invite anyone to forcibly enter my body!

After being raped, my body no longer belonged to me. I was examined to see if I had really been penetrated. To ease the burning, the women smeared salve in my innermost recesses. They looked, they probed, they discussed. Although they wailed and commiserated with me, no one understood me.

My mother and Shechem wanted to solve everything with marriage. My father was impotent with his rage and accusations. My brothers wanted revenge. They all were tearing me apart. My privacy was invaded. I had no place to escape. There was nowhere else to go. No one took my needs into account. I needed to be alone.

They wouldn't let it rest. It rankled and festered like an open wound that would not heal.

My two older brothers, Shimon and Levi, came to me full of plans. They explained their strategy. They were doing it for me. "The honor of the family is at stake," they proclaimed.

"Who cares?" I asked. "Will killing bring about absolution? Will it restore my innocence? Will it free me to love? Will it free me of the fear of being hurt again?"

My brothers set their plans in motion. They ordered me, "Agree to marry Shechem so that peace will be made. The bridal price will be his circumcision."

They plotted to kill Shechem's whole family while they were recovering from the circumcision. His family would be too weak to fight back. The marriage would not take place after all. They sought my approval for this plan.

How ironic! I thought. What a fitting punishment! Mutilate the weapon that ripped me apart. Kill the only person I could marry! Would it make me whole again? Would it erase the memory of the pain? I was young then, I had no power; I let them do what they did. My sentence had been passed.[5] My will to fight was gone. My last act of resistance had been in my cry, "Don't do it!"

Their plan succeeded. They avenged my honor. It was over for them, but not for me. I lie awake at night. Was it the right thing to do? So many lives lost! For what! And the child that later they tore from my body—what became of her? They said they destroyed her—left her to die. She could have united our two families. Then at least my sacrifice would have had some value. We would have had peace in this wretched land.

I still dream about her. They go about their business as if I am invisible. They talk around me, don't look me in the eye. I no longer exist for them. When I walk out of my tent, there is a sudden silence. The topics are changed. I embarrass them. They are afraid to touch me, to draw near.

I register every slight, every nuance of speech. I fear that they are planning some dreadful fate for me. I cringe and hope they will not notice me.

"Poor Dinah, what will become of her?"

---

5. The meaning of *din* is "sentence" or "judgment," as in *gezar din mavet*, "death sentence"; thus, "Dinah" can be understood as "her sentence."

7

TAMAR

Tamar in the Bible

According to Jewish law, if a man died without having children, his brother was obligated to marry his widow and sire children in order to carry on his brother's name. This is known as "levirite marriage." If he refused to do so, a special ritual, called chalitzah, *which required the widow to remove her brother-in-law's sandal and spit in his face, was performed in order to terminate his obligation. Eventually, the Rabbis ruled that the use of* chalitzah *was mandatory and outlawed levirite marriage. However, if the brothers-in-law refuses to perform* chalitzah, *the widow cannot remarry. Onan's choice, to "spill his seed," is also condemned, for while he does marry his brother's wife, he refuses to carry on his brother's name.*

Leila Leah Bronner says, "Tamar actively takes steps to change her destiny, by an act that defies the patriarchal order, in the interest of allowing her, ultimately, to fulfill herself according to its terms."[1] Do you agree with this statement? Do you think Tamar did the right thing?

---

1. Leila Leah Bronner, *From Eve to Esther* (Louisville, KY: Westminister John Knox Press, 1994), p. 153.

About that time Judah left his brothers and camped near a certain Adullamite whose name was Hirah. There Judah saw the daughter of a certain Canaanite whose name was Shua, and he married her and cohabited with her. She conceived and bore a son, and he named him Er. She conceived again and bore a son, and named him Onan. Once again she bore a son, and named him Shelah; he was at Chezib when she bore him.

Judah got a wife for Er his firstborn; her name was Tamar. But Er, Judah's firstborn, was displeasing to the Lord, and the Lord took his life. Then Judah said to Onan, "Join with your brother's wife and do your duty by her as a brother-in-law, and provide offspring for your brother." But Onan, knowing that the seed would not count as his, let it go to waste whenever he joined with his brother's wife, so as not to provide offspring for his brother. What he did was displeasing to the Lord, and He took his life also. Then Judah said to his daughter-in-law Tamar, "Stay as a widow in your father's house until my son Shelah grows up"—for he thought, "He too might die like his brothers." So Tamar went to live in her father's house.

A long time afterward, Shua's daughter, the wife of Judah, died. When his period of mourning was over, Judah went up to Timnah to his sheepshearers, together with his friend Hirah the Adullamite. And Tamar was told, "Your father-in-law is coming up to Timnah for the sheepshearing." So she took off her widow's garb, covered her face with a veil, and, wrapping herself up, sat down at the entrance to Enaim, which is on the road to Timnah; for she saw that Shelah was grown up, yet she had not been given to him as wife. When Judah saw her, he took her for a harlot; for she had covered her face. So he turned aside to her by the road and said, "Here, let me sleep with you"—for he did not know that she was his daughter-in-law. "What," she asked, "will you pay for sleeping with me?" He replied, "I will send a kid from my flock." But she said, "You must leave a pledge until you have sent it." And he said, "What pledge shall I give you?" She replied, "Your seal and cord, and the staff which you carry." So he gave them to her and slept with her, and she conceived by him. Then she went on her way. She took off her veil and again put on her widow's garb.

Judah sent the kid by his friend the Adullamite, to redeem the pledge from the woman; but he could not find her. He inquired of the people of that town, "Where is the cult prostitute, the one at Enaim, by the road?" But they said, "There has been no prostitute here." So he returned to Judah and said, "I could not find her; moreover, the townspeople said: 'There has been no prostitute here.'" Judah said, "Let her keep them, lest we become a laughingstock. I did sent her this kid, but you did not find her."

About three months later, Judah was told, "Your daughter-in-law Tamar has played the harlot; in fact, she is with child by harlotry." "Bring her out," said Judah, "and let her be burned." As she was being brought out, she sent this message to her father-in-law, "I am with child by the man to whom these belong." And she added, "Examine these: whose seal and cord and staff are these?" Judah recognized them, and said, "She is more in the right than I, inasmuch as I did not give her to my son Shelah." And he was not intimate with her again.

When the time came for her to give birth, there were twins in her womb! While she was in labor, one of them put out his hand, and the midwife tied a crimson thread on that hand, to signify: This one came out first. But just then he drew back his hand, and out came his brother; and she said, "What a breach you have made for yourself!" So he was named Perez. Afterward his brother came out, on whose hand was the crimson thread; he was named Zerah (Genesis 38:1–30).

Rabbinic Midrashim

Harlotry is condemned both in the TaNaKH and in the rabbinic sources. Is this view supported in the following midrashim? From whose perspective are they written? Both Tamar and Judah are rewarded. How is this done?

Furthermore, not only was it reported, AND MOREOVER, BEHOLD, SHE IS WITH CHILD BY HARLOTRY [Genesis 38:24], but the text teaches that she would beat upon her stomach and exclaim, I am big with kings and redeemers.[2]

---

2. *Genesis Rabbah* 85:10, in *The Midrash*, ed. and trans. H. Freedman and Maurice Simon et al. (London: Soncino Press, 1951).

Why did God give the crown to Judah? Surely, he was not the only brave one of all his brothers; were not Simeon and Levi and the others valiant too? But because he dealt justly with Tamar did he become judge of the world. . . . [W]hen the case of Tamar came before Judah, under sentence to be burnt, he acquitted her, finding a plea on her behalf. What happened there? Isaac and Jacob and all his brothers sat there trying to screen him, but Judah recognized the place [where he had left his cord, signet and staff] and said, "The thing is correct; SHE IS MORE RIGHTEOUS THAN I" [Genesis 38:26]. For this, God made him a prince.[3]

R. Samuel b. Naḥmani [said] in the name of R. Jonathan: Every bride who is modest in the house of her father-in-law is rewarded by having kings and prophets among her descendants. How do we prove this? From Tamar, as it is written, AND JUDAH SAW HER AND THOUGHT HER TO BE A HARLOT; FOR SHE HAD COVERED HER FACE [Genesis 38:15]. Now because she had covered her face did he think her to be a harlot? Rather, what it means is that because she had covered her face in the house of her father-in-law and he did not know her, she was rewarded by having among her descendants kings and prophets.[4]

Tamar

by Ingrid Hughes

Ingrid Hughes retells Tamar's story through her eyes in "Tamar." Why, according to this story, did she choose to do what she did? Was this question answered in the biblical narrative? What motivation did the Rabbis assume? How does this story affect the way you understand Tamar?

3. *Exodus Rabbah* 38:26, in ibid.

4. Babylonian Talmud, *Megillah* 10b, in *The Babylonian Talmud*, ed. and trans. I. Epstein et al. (London: Soncino Press, 1935–1952).

Judah was tender with Hagar the winter she was sick. Her flesh shrank away from her bones and her eyes burned, avid and angry. He carried her from her tent himself and set her on her pillows under the olive trees, holding her hands as she muttered. Her life had been cruel, she said. She had brought forth three sons, and two of them had died before her. If she caught sight of me, she would say, "It's the fault of that one that I have no grandchildren."

"Hagar, that's not just," Judah would say. For a moment he would look aside, then his whitening eyes might rest on my breasts before he lifted his chin and pointed his beard toward my father's tents on the other side of the spring, to send me back home.

I would slip away, furious and crying. Didn't she see that I too was bereft? She had lain with a man, borne children, held them to her breasts. She was a woman of rank, to whom others deferred, whose husband was tending her even as she lay dying. No such fortune had been mine. I was nobody's wife and nobody's mother, forever at the fringes, waved away. Yet it had all been promised me by Judah, when his eyes were clear and he picked me out for his first son, picked me for my beauty and my virtues and my strength to continue the royal line. "She's good-natured," he had said, telling my parents why he wanted me. "She will accept the will of the Mighty One." He said this because I had grown up at his feet, where my brothers and sisters and cousins all scrambled in the sand with his sons, within the moving circles of tents.

So Judah chose me for Er, who was so handsome I could hardly look at his face, son of the chieftain, seed of Jacob. I agreed, my parents settled on the bride-price, and I was ready. My mother and father took me to Judah's tents and gave me to Er.

That evening as we all feasted, Er's eyes were on me, eager and excited. His glance danced away and then back. My gaze clung to them, dark pools I wanted to enter. I waited impatiently for everyone else to go. But when we entered our tent, I saw by the oil burning in the jar that his skin was almost gray. His lips were blue. I took his hand and his palm was wet. Terrified, I watched him collapse helplessly, shuddering and thrashing. His eyes found mine for one last moment, and then closed. I ran from the tent screaming, and his parents came. All night they sat with him, and before dawn he stopped breathing. While they kept vigil I clung to the girl who had been given me as my maid, Rebecca. We rocked together while his mother wailed that the Mighty One was cruel, and Judah paced and cried. After Er was buried, in the morning, I cried too, even more frightened than saddened by my loss.

We mourned for endless weeks. I would walk away as far as I could and lie behind a rock or tree all day, my mouth dry, a haze of confusion and fear like a weight on my body, as I dozed and woke and waited for evening. When I returned I had to listen to Hagar. "Why?" she would ask over and over. Nobody could answer her. We all knew Er must have done something terrible for his life to end that way. Usually He takes the lives of the old, or warriors, or babies whose breath is still uncertain. Rarely does He take a healthy youth. "My son was a good man," Hagar would yell, up toward the heavens. "Why am I suffering when other mothers' sons thrive?"

Judah often went to walk in the fields with the shepherd. One evening he returned and found us sitting outside the tents under the tree while Hagar ranted. He sat down and placed his large hand on her neck.

"We must accept this. It's not right to resist the Mighty One," he said sadly. I respected him because he could see beyond himself and his pain.

"This is my decision," he said. "Onan will be Tamar's husband." I turned to Onan, fearing something would go wrong again. During the weeks of mourning he had been silent and remote, as indeed he had been all the years we were growing up. Then he used to play by himself, scratching in the sand with a stick, piling stones into shapes he told us other children we wouldn't understand.

This time there was a quiet meal; we didn't want to attract the attention of the Almighty One. We were lying together already when he asked me, "Do you want to have my child?"

"Yes, I do, I want a child," I said.

"But it won't be mine, it will be my brother's. I only got you because my seed is the seed of Judah, son of Jacob," he said bitterly. He put his hand on my bare breast. "You weren't chosen for me. You didn't agree to marry me."

"Your brother was never my husband," I said. I was bewildered. Of course, I was the wife of his brother—but now his by right, wasn't that enough? Son of Jacob and Judah, how could he be more?

"I want my own wife and my own son," he said.

"I am your wife. I will bear your son."

"You are beautiful." He kissed me then, and I began to feel easier. But when he thrust into me again and again I was in pain and I wanted him to stop. Soon he reared back and pulled himself from within me so that his seed spilled on the ground.

"Why did you do that?" I knew this was wrong. Now I couldn't conceive a child.

"I had to," he said. "I can't be the ram brought in to the best ewe. I will be myself, Onan, no matter what." He rose and wrapped himself in his robes and passed into the cold night. I cried with frustration, and lay alone dreading the morning. When it was light a shepherd found his body, bitten by a small snake as he walked in the night, the snake crushed in his fist. I had to tell Judah what had happened before his death. "Poor girl," Judah said, and put his arm on my shoulder. I held on to his warm body, comforting and sturdy, and he began to sob. He let go of me and went to tell Hagar. This time we knew what the wickedness was. Again we talked of Er, and Hagar asked me over and over if I knew why he had died. Judah asked me too. In my sleep they continued to question me, and I woke frightened many nights, my heart pounding.

"I didn't know Er," I said each time they questioned me. "He was your son."

Finally Judah said, "Go back to your father's tents and remain a widow till little Shelah is old enough to marry you, if the Almighty is willing."

My maid Rebecca went with me to my father's. "Sad Tamar," she would say, "Sad Tamar." I never told her how I worried that the Mighty One was against me.

My older brother's wife had a new baby at the breast, though her first son was almost ready to take a wife. The baby looked into the eyes of my sister-in-law, and she looked into his, as I had looked into Er's during the night of feasting. As this baby grew he still came to her, tugged at her robes till she opened them, and held one of his hands to her breast while he sucked. My breasts would burn with longing at the sight.

"Go away now," she would say to me, seeing my eyes. Banished, I would go behind the tents and stroke my breasts, but my skin burned more, and I grew more hungry, not less.

"Tamar stares at me too much," my brother's wife told him. He frowned at me. By now they didn't have to think of my sorrow. I was another helper, little different from my Rebecca, my most frequent companion, except that Rebecca had married a shepherd and was a mother herself, so that often it was I who helped her. She at least didn't forbid me to look at her with longing, though sometimes she said, "Tamar, you pain me. Here, take the child." I would hold her daughter, but I couldn't comfort her.

Now years had passed, Rebecca had five children, and Hagar was an old woman, dying, with no grandchildren. Judah had not kept his promise that Shelah would beget my children. I put myself in his way on the path to the spring.

"Judah, I am growing older," I said, as he came near. He nodded his covered head with silent formality, as if he had already considered this and set it aside, without breaking his stride down the hill. He had decided to forget me, let me live my life without the daily wheat and honey of husband or children, without a family of my own to include me in the circle of life it formed, without sons or daughters to join me to the coming generations. Bitterly, I considered my situation and determined I would make Judah keep his promise.

Judah had never taken a concubine, perhaps because the sorrow of their dead sons bound him to Hagar. When Hagar was gone he would be full of lust. Once in my girlhood when we passed by the gates of a strange village, a woman had been sitting alone on a rock, her face veiled, talking to the men who went by. I was startled. She had nothing to sell, so what could she talk to strangers about? My mother said she was a harlot, who sold her own body, as the Egyptians did.

"Why?" I asked. My mother had told me there was always a reason for wickedness.

"Maybe her family died and she is alone."

Remembering that woman, I decided that after Hagar's death I would take off the mourning I had promised to wear as the widow of Judah's sons and sit outside the gates of Enaim on the road I knew Judah would take to the sheepshearing in the spring.

Hagar withered yet more. Now she was skin clinging to bones, nearly a skeleton. I watched from a distance. She ate no more than a bite or two of food, swallowed a mouthful of water, then pushed it away.

I explained my plan to Rebecca, for I would need her help. She gasped when I told her what I meant to do. "You must wait for Shelah.

He's grown tall and handsome, old enough to marry. Judah promised him to you."

I shook my head. "Judah won't talk to me. He does not intend to keep his promise."

"He will. You are impatient. After Hagar dies he will."

"I am sure he will not. Shelah will not marry me—he is a young man, too young."

"Approach him, ask him. That would not be so terrible as what you plan."

I shook my head.

"If Shelah won't anger Judah, who are you to dare?"

"I am more desperate than Shelah. Let Judah be angry. Let the Almighty strike me down. Better than living my life like this," I cried out, my anger making me strong.

"Judah will punish you. You can't shame him publicly."

"He broke his promise to me," I said. I went to sit by myself under a palm tree.

I was afraid. First of the Mighty One. Er and Onan had died for their wickedness. Rebecca was right, I might be killed too. Do I want to die? I whispered to myself. I began to sob with fear. When I quieted I thought again of the children I was meant to bring forth. I was in the right. I knew that. I would go ahead.

Hagar died. Judah and Shelah buried her. The weeks passed, Judah resumed his herding, the spring sun grew strong, and one evening my father said that Judah was going to the sheepshearing in a few days. So Rebecca and I slipped away to the spring, and she washed my hair and lined my eyes with kohl. She rubbed my breasts and neck and ear lobes with oil and myrrh. We left my father's tents early in the dark morning while everyone still slept, and when the sun was beginning to rise we stopped at a grove. Rebecca took the torn robes I had grown to hate and gave me a plain, new robe and veil. Then she went back to my father's to say I was sick and staying in her tent.

I walked along the sandy trail, watching the birds fly up from the bushes as I approached, and growing hot as the sun rose in the sky. When I reached the gates of Enaim I had to sit waiting for hours, turning away from the whistles and propositions of other men.

"Why are you sitting there if you're too good for me?" one shepherd said angrily, when I refused to raise my face to his. I'm not selling myself, I'm getting my due, I thought. Still, my heart beat like a gong in my chest, my body shuddered, and I had to go over the rightness of it all with myself again.

At last, in the late afternoon, Judah came, with his friend Hirah, the Adullamite, and their men, on their way to the sheepshearing. Judah left Hirah and came up as soon as he saw me. I had judged right, he was full of lust.

"Good afternoon, woman," he said very politely. "I'd like you to come to my tent tonight." His voice wasn't easy when he said this.

My courage ebbed, and I dropped my head, afraid he would know me when I spoke. If he did, he would be shamed; he wouldn't go through with it. But I must speak. It would be all for nothing if I didn't make sure of his tokens. "To your tent? What will you give me?" I asked.

He showed no sign of recognition at the sound of my voice. "I'll send you a kid as soon as I have one that's ready to leave its mother," he said. A kid was a handsome payment; too much, I thought. But I kept bargaining.

"I need something to show you mean it," I said.

"Yes, of course." He removed his seal from his finger, and then gave me the band on his head that showed he was a chief. I was shocked to be holding these in my hands, and he misunderstood my hesitation.

"Take my staff as well," he said.

"Thank you," I said. "Thank you. Thank you."

"Come to my tent after dark," he said, and walked back to Hirah. So after dark I went to the place where his men had set up his tent on the other side of the gates. Again my body had become a drum for my heart to beat against.

"Let me in," I said, at the opening to his tent. "Here's the staff you gave me."

"Come in," he said. He was alone. I was frightened as I took off the veil. But he gave my face only a quick glance, and then began to remove his own robes. He still didn't recognize me. I was relieved by the girth of his strong body, aging, unlike the slender youths Er and Onan. I lay down on the mat, watching him as he began to stroke my breasts, almost absentmindedly, and showed his pleasure. My bitterness seemed to lie like a fine dust on my skin, so his hand passing over me made me burn with anger and excitement at once.

Now you get me with child, I told myself, closing my eyes. I felt his hard probing between my legs then, and was frightened. How could he look at me without recognizing me? Was I no longer Tamar, but a harlot, as he thought? Blind old man, I told myself, you blind old liar.

"Your heart is strong," he said, his head on my chest. He entered into me, and this time it didn't hurt. My groin seemed to turn into an animal, running and thrashing, and I heard in my own words, blind old liar, blind old lion, till he moaned, and I whimpered, and he slept. I lay quietly next to him, sleepless, not allowing myself any thoughts. When he woke I touched him, to excite him again. I wanted more seed. This was my only chance.

"You will have two sons," he said, when he had moaned again. I waited without moving, wanted the seed to take root. After a long time I knew the sun must be about to rise. I left then, taking the seal, the cord, and the staff. I walked quickly away from Enaim, so as not to be seen, back along the track, hungry and thirsty and aching, till I met Rebecca in the grove. She gave me my own robes, and I put them on, thinking, not for long now. Together we returned to my father's tents.

For days my body grew warm when I thought of what I had done. Yet I felt less angry, almost tender, when Judah returned from his sheep-shearing. My hands shook so much I was afraid my mother would notice, and each time I heard a noise I jumped. But as time passed I understood that my deed would not be known until my parents saw I was carrying a child.

One morning I saw Hirah leaving the encampment with a new kid under his arm. I laughed to think that he was going to Enaim to give the prostitute her due. They would say, "What harlot? There's no harlot here." But in the evening I was sad when I saw him come back. I had tricked Judah. His anger would be great when he learned the truth.

The pomegranates were ripe when my mother finally saw that my breasts were swollen and my belly was round. She wept and my father turned on me. "Judah will decide what should be done with you," he said.

"I will accept his judgment," I said.

"He told you to wait for Shelah."

"I waited many years."

"How did it happen?" he wailed. "How? Tell me!"

"I cannot tell you," I said. I cried because he wouldn't understand.

"You are no longer my daughter," my father said. He took me to where Judah was standing in the open between his tents. My father told Judah I had gotten with child, like a harlot. The hot wind swept across the desert and blew my robes against my belly.

"Tamar has prostituted herself," Judah said, respecting my father's news. His face was a refusal, blank and shocked.

I filled with rage. "Look at me, Judah; don't you recognize me?" I said.

"The penalty for prostitution is death," he said. I saw my mother weaken and stagger. My father held her.

"Before you judge me, let me give you something to know me by." I pulled his possessions from my robes. He took his seal, band, and staff and looked at them, and looked at me, and saw me for the first time since he had chosen me for Er.

"Tamar, the harlot from the gates of Enaim," he said, his face aghast.

"You promised I would bear Jacob's sons." My mother and father were silent. I stood numbly in the sun, supported by nothing but the hot wind. Judah paced, holding the staff, his robes blowing. Then he stood still.

"I broke my promise to give her to Shelah. Tamar is more righteous than I," he told my father and mother. "She will come to live in my tents now."

When my time came I labored for many hours. It was so difficult that the midwife knew I was going to have twins. But they were tangled together and couldn't get out. Then one thrust his hand out, and the midwife tied a thread around it to show that he was first. He pulled his arm in and the other came first. In this, as in everything, we were out of order.

When the midwife had taken the babies to bathe them, I lay resting in the twilight. Judah came near. "Remember you said I would have twins?" I asked him. We had never spoken of the night that I conceived.

"Yes, I remember."

Judah was always respectful, formal, almost afraid of me. He lived for another ten years, to watch his sons grow. He sent me honey and nuts in the mornings. He brought me meat in the evenings. I never let another woman suckle my sons, but held Perez to one breast, Zerah to the other, and watched their small mouths pump. I dressed them myself, held them to me, and took counsel with Judah about who their wives should be, before he died.

Now their wives live in tents near mine, and defy those who talk about my past, by bringing their children to me for advice. They hold my wisdom to be great. They don't understand that my courage came not only from righteousness, but from my powerful need, and my resolve to satisfy it.

8

MIRIAM

Miriam in the Bible

Although she is not named in her first appearance, Miriam is Moses' sister. (It is important to note that none of the other individuals in that narrative—except Moses—are named, either.) As far as we know from the text, Miriam never marries nor does she have children.

How would you characterize Miriam as we first see her, as big sister to the infant Moses? What was she like at the Red Sea? She was part of the leadership team during Israel's wanderings, but was she equal to Moses—or to Aaron? How do you think she felt about the incident at Hazeroth? Do you think she was guilty as charged? Would Miriam have led the women in dancing at the shore of the sea had she known then what would happen there?

A certain man of the house of Levi went and married a Levite woman. The woman conceived and bore a son; and when she saw how beautiful he was, she hid him for three months. When she could hide him no longer, she got a wicker basket for him and caulked it with bitumen and pitch. She put the child into it and placed it among the reeds by the bank of the Nile. And his sister stationed herself at a distance, to learn what would befall him.

The daughter of Pharaoh came down to bathe in the Nile, while her maidens walked along the Nile. She spied the basket among the reeds and sent her slave girl to fetch it. When she opened it, she saw that it was a child, a boy crying. She took pity on it and said, "This must be a Hebrew child." Then his sister said to Pharaoh's daughter, "Shall I go and get you a Hebrew nurse to suckle the child for you?" And Pharaoh's daughter answered, "Yes." So the girl went and called the child's mother. And Pharaoh's daughter said to her, "Take this child and nurse it for me, and I will pay your wages." So the woman took the child and nursed it. When the child grew up, she brought him to Pharaoh's daughter, who made him her son. She named him Moses, explaining, "I drew him out of the water" (Exodus 2:1–10).

. . . Then Moses held out his arm over the sea and the Lord drove back the sea with a strong east wind all that night, and turned the sea into dry ground. The waters were split, and the Israelites went into the sea on dry ground, the waters forming a wall for them on their right and on their left. The Egyptians came in pursuit after them into the sea, all of Pharaoh's horses, chariots, and horsemen. At the morning watch, the Lord looked down upon the Egyptian army from a pillar of fire and cloud, and threw the Egyptian army into panic. He locked the wheels of their chariots so that they moved forward with difficulty. And the Egyptians said, "Let us flee from the Israelites, for the Lord is fighting for them against Egypt."

Then the Lord said to Moses, "Hold out your arm over the sea, that the waters may come back upon the Egyptians and upon their chariots and upon their horsemen." Moses held out his arm over the sea, and at daybreak the sea returned to its normal state, and the Egyptians fled at its approach. But the Lord hurled the Egyptians into the sea. The waters turned back and covered the chariots and the horsemen—Pharaoh's entire army that followed them into the sea; not one of them remained. But the Israelites had marched through the sea on dry ground, the waters forming a wall for them on their right and on their left (Exodus 14:21–29).

. . . Then Moses and the Israelites sang this song to the Lord. They said:

"I will sing to the Lord, for He has triumphed gloriously;
Horse and driver He has hurled into the sea . . ." (Exodus 15:1).

. . . Then Miriam the prophetess, Aaron's sister, took a timbrel in her hand, and all the women went out after her in dance with timbrels. And Miriam chanted for them:

Sing to the Lord, for He has triumphed gloriously;
Horse and driver he has hurled into the sea. (Exodus 15:20–21).

. . . When they were in Hazeroth, Miriam and Aaron spoke against Moses because of the Cushite woman he had married: "He married a Cushite woman!"

They said, "Has the Lord spoken only through Moses? Has He not spoken through us as well?" The Lord heard it. Now Moses was a very humble man, more so than any other man on earth. Suddenly the Lord called to Moses, Aaron, and Miriam, "Come out, you three, to the Tent of Meeting." So the three of them went out. The Lord came down in a pillar of cloud, stopped at the entrance of the Tent, and called out, "Aaron and Miriam!" The two of them came forward; and He said, "Hear these My words: When a prophet of the Lord arises among you, I make Myself known to him in a vision, I speak with him in a dream. Not so with My servant Moses; he is trusted throughout My household. With him I speak mouth to mouth, plainly and not in riddles, and he beholds the likeness of the Lord. How then did you not shrink from speaking against My servant Moses!" Still incensed with them, the Lord departed.

As the cloud withdrew from the Tent, there was Miriam stricken with snow-white scales. When Aaron turned toward Miriam, he saw that she was stricken with scales. And Aaron said to Moses, "O my lord, account not to us the sin which we committed in our folly. Let her not be as one dead, who emerges from his mother's womb with half his flesh eaten away." So Moses cried out to the Lord, saying, "O God, pray heal her!"

But the Lord said to Moses, "If her father spat in her face, would she not bear her shame for seven days? Let her be shut out of camp for seven days, and then let her be readmitted." So Miriam was shut out of camp seven days; and the people did not march on until Miriam was readmitted (Numbers 12:1–15).

. . . The Israelites arrived in a body at the wilderness of Zin on the first new moon, and the people stayed at Kadesh. Miriam died there and was buried there (Numbers 20:1).

Rabbinic Midrashim

In the TaNaKH we see Miriam in several roles, and these midrashim comment on them. How do they characterize Miriam's role in Moses' early life? What aspect of Miriam's story most concerns them? Which aspect were you most drawn to? Which of Miriam's actions merited praise, according to the Rabbis? How, according to them, did her outspokenness relate to those actions?

AND MIRIAM THE PROPHETESS . . . TOOK . . . [Exodus 15:20]. But where do we find that Miriam prophesied? It is merely this: Miriam had said to her father: "You are destined to beget a son who will arise and save Israel from the hands of the Egyptians." Immediately, THERE WENT A MAN OF THE HOUSE OF LEVI AND TOOK TO WIFE . . . AND THE WOMAN CONCEIVED AND BORE A SON AND WHEN SHE COULD NO LONGER HIDE HIM, ETC. [Exodus 2:1–3]. Then her father reproached her. He said to her: "Miriam! What of thy prediction?" But she still held on to her prophecy, as it is said: AND HIS SISTER STOOD AFAR OFF, TO KNOW WHAT WOULD BE DONE TO HIM [ibid., 2:4].[1]

AND MIRIAM SANG UNTO THEM [Exodus 15:21]. Scripture tells that just as Moses recited the song for the men, so Miriam recited the song for the women: SING YE TO THE LORD, FOR HE IS HIGHLY EXALTED, ETC. [ibid.].[2]

The Rabbis say: The words SUFFER NOT THY MOUTH TO BRING THY FLESH INTO GUILT [Ecclesiastes 5:5] are addressed to

---

1. *Mekhilta de-Rabbi Ishmael*, *Shirata* 10:58–65, in *Mekhilta de-Rabbi Ishmael*, trans. Jacob Z. Lauterbach (Philadelphia: Jewish Publication Society, 1949).

2. *Mekhilta de-Rabbi Ishmael*, *Shirata* 10:89–91, in ibid.

Miriam. As soon as she spoke against Moses, she became leprous, for it is said MIRIAM AND AARON SPOKE AGAINST MOSES [Numbers 12:1]. And what happened to her? AND BEHOLD MIRIAM BECAME LEPROUS, WHITE AS SNOW [ibid., 12:10]. NEITHER SAY THOU BEFORE THE MESSENGER [Ecclesiastes 5:5]: before Moses. WHERE-FORE SHOULD GOD BE ANGRY AT THY VOICE [ibid.], the voice that Miriam let escape from her mouth against Moses the righteous. AND DESTROY THE WORK OF THY HANDS [ibid.]—that is, destroy the merit of her timbrel-playing, of which it is said AND MIRIAM THE PROPHETESS, THE SISTER OF AARON, TOOK A TIMBREL IN HER HAND [Exodus 15:20].[3]

Another comment: REMEMBER [Deuteronomy 24:9]. The rabbis say: This can be compared to a king who returned [in triumph] from war, and a noble lady sang his praises, and the king decreed that she should be called the Mother of the Senate. Later, she began to cause disorder in the royal provisions. Said the king thereupon: "Is that what she does? Let her be sent away to the mines." So, when God waged war at the Red Sea, Miriam chanted a song, and she was named prophetess, as it is said, AND MIRIAM THE PROPHETESS . . . TOOK . . . [Exodus 15:20]. When, however, she slandered her brother, God commanded that she should be sent to the mines, as it is said, AND MIRIAM WAS SHUT UP [Numbers 12:15].[4]

The Discredited Prophetess
by Naomi Graetz[5]

In "The Discredited Prophetess," is Naomi Graetz commenting only on Miriam? Do you think the Rabbis were commenting on broader issues? Do you

---

3. "The Midrash on Psalms 52:1," in *The Midrash on Psalms*, trans. William G. Braude (New Haven, CT: Yale University Press, 1959).

4. *Deuteronomy Rabbah* 6:12, in *The Midrash*, ed. and trans. H. Freedman and Maurice Simon et al. (London: Soncino Press, 1951).

5. This midrash appears in a longer version in the *Melton Journal*, Fall 1987, p. 10.

agree that men and women view God differently—worship differently? How
might Judaism have been different had Miriam been Moses' equal partner?
What if she, instead of Moses, had led Israel out of Egypt?

[And] Miriam was stricken with snow-white scales . . . [and she] was
shut out of camp for seven days; but the people did not march on until
Miriam was readmitted (Numbers 12:10–15).

This is much worse than I thought! I must find something to do. It was the
morning of her third day of banishment.

Why must those who are diseased expiate their sin by spending the entire
period alone—separated from others similarly afflicted? What kind of God
demands that one endure this mental and physical pain in a state of loneliness!

Miriam met people with different skin diseases, yet each person's
complaint was the loneliness.

"Why not get together and take care of each other? Put up makeshift
huts for those who are really sick. The healthy people can care for the
very sick," she suggested. She realized that she had reinterpreted the law
of badad yeshev, "you shall remain in complete isolation."[6] I hope I won't
be punished for usurping Moses' power of interpretation. She was well aware
of the danger of stepping out of line, having witnessed God's wrath many
times.

Why wasn't Aaron similarly afflicted? Is criticism of our brother now to be
tabooed?

Miriam felt that she or Aaron would have been equally qualified to
lead the people out of Egypt and had never accepted God's choice of
Moses.

Perhaps I wasn't chosen because I am a woman. Is it God who does not
want women to worship Him? Or is it those who claim to speak in His name,
who control the power, who do not want women to worship Him?

She asked this because the leaders, who were all men, described God
as an all-powerful and vengeful being. But women, she knew, thought

---

6. Leviticus 13:46.

God was caring and compassionate. Men had decreed that women be excluded from holy work and had elected priests to formulate laws that treated women with contempt.

We are children in their eyes. I remember when it was different.

In Egypt, the women's nurturing talents were essential, because the men were physically exhausted and emotionally drained from their demeaning work as slaves. The women played musical instruments and worshipped the *terafim*, the household gods of their ancestresses in Ur.

The new form of religion was deliberately dry and abstract. Women were not allowed into the holy area, because their form of worship was too spontaneous and earthy in contrast to the new formal rituals. *No wonder our people needed a golden calf to worship.*

Miriam felt it was wrong of God to command mankind not to make any graven images of Him. He had killed hundreds of His people simply for their needing a concretized version of Him in the form of a Golden Calf to feel and touch.

We were not ready to accede to His demand that we accept an intangible essence and call it God. We had not left the mental state of slavery. We needed compassion and understanding when we failed to observe the first commandment, but were expected instead to be satisfied with divine wrath and displays of power.

She had given much to this people. She had raised and advised its leader. When their fledgling nation succeeded in fleeing Pharaoh's army, she had composed a song for the occasion. It was immediately after the singing of her Song of the Sea that the people started calling her *marah*, bitter, making puns of her name. She thought that one day they would no doubt call her song, "*shirat Mar-yam*," song of the bitter sea!

Was I bitter then? Or was it after we were unable to get sweet water, when Moses implied that it was my fault that the waters were bitter?

She felt that it was going to be difficult to worship a God who afflicted people with diseases for not agreeing with Him. *Is it Moses or God who makes these decisions? Does it matter? It does! For this is not the God I left Egypt to worship. I cannot accept that this is God's doing. That was why He saw to it that I was punished. It was only after Aaron cried out in protest that Moses cried out, "O Lord, please heal her!" Would he have done so earlier?*

It is lonely here. Four more days to go.

9

THE DAUGHTERS OF ZELOPHEHAD

The Daughters of Zelophehad in the Bible

Moses and the elders decided legal issues in accordance with the laws of the Torah. For Moses to take a case to God suggests that the issues involved were too complex or controversial for the elders to resolve. Laws concerning the hereditary disposition of land had already been given, but did not address a situation in which there were no male heirs. What does this suggest to you about biblical lawmaking? How does the ruling impact the economic status of women?

Are you surprised that a group of very young women approached Moses directly? Why do you think they went as a delegation? The sisters' names are listed three times. Why is this so when other women of the Bible (i.e., Lot's wife and Jephthah's daughter) are nameless?

Descendants of Manasseh: Of Machir, the clan of the Machirites.--Machir begot Gilead.--Of Gilead, the clan of the Gileadites. These were the descendants of Gilead: [Of] Iezer, the clan of the Iezerites; of Helek, the clan of the Helekites; [of] Asriel, the clan of the Asrielites; [of] Shechem, the clan of the Shechemites; [of] Shemida, the clan of the Shemidaites; [of] Hepher, the clan of the Hepherites.--Now Zelophehad son of Hepher had no sons, only daughters. The names of Zelophehad's daughters were Mahlah, Noah, Hoglah, Milcah, and Tirzah.—Those are the clans of Manasseh; persons enrolled: 52,700 (Numbers 26:29–34).

. . . The daughters of Zelophehad, of Manassite family—son of Hepher son of Gilead son of Machir son of Manasseh son of Joseph—came forward. The names of the daughters were Mahlah, Noah, Hoglah, Milcah, and Tirzah. They stood before Moses, Eleazer the priest, the chieftains, and the whole assembly, at the entrance to the Tent of Meeting, and they said, "Our father died in the wilderness. He was not one of the faction, Korah's faction, which banded together against the Lord, but died for his own sin; and he has left no sons. Let not our father's name be lost to his clan just because he had no son! Give us a holding among our father's kinsmen!"

Moses brought their case before the Lord.

And the Lord said to Moses, "The plea of Zelophehad's daughters is just: you should give them a hereditary holding among their father's kinsmen; transfer their father's share to them.

"Further, speak to the Israelite people as follows: 'If a man dies without leaving a son, you shall transfer his property to his daughter. If he has no daughter, you shall assign his property to his brothers. If he has no brothers, you shall assign his property to his father's brothers. If his father had no brothers, you shall assign his property to his nearest relative in his own clan, and he shall inherit it.' This shall be the law of procedure for the Israelites, in accordance with the Lord's command to Moses" (Numbers 27:1–11).

. . . The family heads in the clan of the descendants of Gilead son of Machir son of Manasseh, one of the Josephite clans, came forward and appealed to Moses and the chieftains, family heads of the Israelites. They said, "The Lord commanded my lord to assign the land to the Israelites as shares by lot, and my lord was further commanded by the Lord to assign the share of our kinsman Zelophehad to his daughters. Now, if they marry persons from another Israelite tribe, their share will be cut off from our ancestral portion and be added to the portion of the tribe into which they marry; thus our allotted portion will be diminished. And even when the Israelites observe the jubilee, their share will be added to that of the tribe into which they marry, and their share will be cut off from the ancestral portion of our tribe."

So Moses, at the Lord's bidding, instructed the Israelites, saying: "The plea of the Josephite tribe is just. This is what the Lord has commanded concerning the daughters of Zelophehad: They may marry anyone they wish, provided they marry into a clan of their father's tribe. No inheritance of the Israelites may pass over from one tribe to another, but the Israelites must remain bound each to the ancestral portion of his tribe. Every daughter among the Israelite tribes who inherits a share must marry someone from a clan of her father's tribe, in order that every Israelite may keep his ancestral share. Thus no inheritance shall pass over from one tribe to another, but the Israelite tribes shall remain bound each to its portion."

The daughters of Zelophehad did as the Lord commanded Moses: Mahlah, Tirzah, Hoglah, Milcah, and Noah, Zelophehad's daughters, were married to sons of their uncles, marrying into clans of descendants of Manasseh son of Joseph; and so their share remained in the tribe of their father's clan (Numbers 36:1–12).

Rabbinic Midrashim

For what qualities do the Rabbis praise the Daughters of Zelophehad? What do you think of the second midrash's statement about the attitudes of men toward women? Do you agree with this assessment of men—with this assessment of God? What do you think Mahlah, Noah, Hoglah, Milcah, and Tirzah discussed when they "gathered to take counsel"?

THEN DREW NEAR THE DAUGHTERS OF ZELOPHEHAD, ETC. [Numbers 27:1]. It was a distinction to them as well as to their father; it was distinction also to Machir as well as to Joseph, that such women issued from them. They were wise and righteous women. What shows their wisdom? They spoke at the appropriate moment, for Moses was engaged upon the subject of inheritances, saying: UNTO THESE THE LAND SHALL BE DIVIDED [Numbers 26:53].[1]

1. *Numbers Rabbah* 21:11, in *The Midrash*, ed. and trans. H. Freedman and Maurice Simon et al. (London: Soncino Press, 1951).

THEN DREW NEAR THE DAUGHTERS OF ZELOPHEHAD,
ETC. (Numbers 27:1). When the daughters of Zelophehad heard that the
land was about to be divided among the tribes—but only for males, not
for females—they gathered to take counsel. They decided that the
mercies of flesh and blood are not like the mercies of Him who is
everywhere. Flesh and blood is apt to be more merciful to males than to
females. But He who spoke and the world came into being is different—
His mercies are for males as well as females, His mercies being for all:
THE LORD IS GOOD TO ALL, AND HIS TENDER MERCIES ARE
OVER ALL HIS WORKS [Psalms 145:9].

GIVE UNTO US A POSSESSION [Numbers 27:4]. R. Nathan said:
Women's tenacity is stronger than men's. The men of Israel [being willing
to give up the Land], said LET US MAKE A CAPTAIN AND LET US
RETURN TO EGYPT (Numbers 14:4). But Israel's women insisted,
GIVE US A POSSESSION.[2]

Davar Aher *(Another Interpretation)*

by Naomi Hyman

*"Davar Aher" draws on traditional forms to express contemporary ideas.
Does the form adequately convey the message? Does the message seem
appropriate to the form? What are some of the advantages and disadvantages
of using traditional forms for contemporary purposes?*

At the beginning of Bemidbar, the Holy One, blessed be, commands
Moses to TAKE A CENSUS OF THE WHOLE ISRAELITE
COMMUNITY . . . LISTING THE NAMES, EVERY *MALE*, HEAD
BY HEAD [Numbers 1:2, emphasis added]. And what do we find?

---

2. *Sifre Numbers* 133, in *The Book of Legends*. ed. Hayim Nahman Bialik and
Yehoshua Hana Ravnitzky; trans. William G. Braude (New York: Schocken
Books, 1992).

THE PEOPLE TOOK TO COMPLAINING BITTERLY [ibid., 11:1], THE
WHOLE COMMUNITY BROKE INTO LOUD CRIES, AND THE
PEOPLE WEPT THAT NIGHT [ibid., 14:1], NOW KORACH SON
OF LEVI, BETOOK HIMSELF . . . TO RISE UP AGAINST MOSES
TOGETHER WITH TWO HUNDRED AND FIFTY ISRAELITES,
CHIEFTAINS OF THE COMMUNITY [ibid., 16:1] and THE PEOPLE
PROFANED THEMSELVES WITH WHORING WITH THE MO-
ABITE WOMEN [ibid., 25:1]. At the end of Bemidbar, the Holy One
Blessed be also commands a census and we find in it the names of women:
THE NAMES OF ZELOPHEHAD'S DAUGHTERS WERE MAHLAH,
NOAH, HOGLAH, MILCAH, AND TIRZAH [ibid., 26:33] and THE
NAME OF ASHER'S DAUGHTER WAS SERAH [ibid., 26:46]. And
what do we find? THE PLEA OF THE DAUGHTERS OF ZELOPHE-
HAD IS JUST [ibid., 27:7] and THE DAUGHTERS OF ZELOPHE-
HAD DID AS THE LORD HAD COMMANDED [ibid., 36:10].

Why do we find the names of the Daughters of Zelophehad listed not
once, but four times [Numbers 26:33, 27:1, 36:10, Joshua 17:3]? This is to
teach us that when we speak up for ourselves, we claim the right to name
the world as we see it. Another interpretation: This is to remind us that
women are important not only in relation to their families, but as
individuals as well, as it is said: THE NAMES OF ZELOPHEHAD'S
DAUGHTERS WERE MAHLAH, NOAH, HOGLAH, MILCAH,
AND TIRZAH [Numbers 26:33].

10

DEBORAH

Deborah in the Bible

As you read this account, notice the way in which the text introduces Deborah. What words are used to portray her? What kind of actions does she take? What is the tone of her statements? How is she perceived in this text?

The long poem at the end of this narrative is known as Deborah's song. It is thought to be one of the oldest such Hebrew poems. Some suggest that the many female images in the song indicate that it was written by a woman.

Is Deborah a good role model? How do you think she will be portrayed in the rabbinic midrashim?

~❦~

The Israelites again did what was offensive to the Lord. . . . And the Lord surrendered them to King Jabin of Canaan, who reigned in Hazor. His army commander was Sisera, whose base was Harosheth-goiim. The Israelites cried out to the Lord; for he had nine hundred iron chariots, and he had oppressed Israel ruthlessly for twenty years.

Deborah, wife of Lappidoth, was a prophetess; she led Israel at that time. She used to sit under the Palm of Deborah, between Ramah and Bethel in the hill country of Ephraim, and the Israelites would come to her for decisions.

She summoned Barak son of Abinoam, of Kedesh in Naphtali, and said to him, "The Lord, the God of Israel, has commanded: Go, march up to Mount Tabor, and take with you ten thousand men of Naphtali and Zebulun. And I will draw Sisera, Jabin's army commander, with his chariots and his troops, toward you up to the Wadi Kishon; and I will deliver him into your hands." But Barak said to her, "If you will go with me, I will go; if not, I will not go." "Very well, I will go with you," she answered. "However, there will be no glory for you in the course you are taking, for then the Lord will deliver Sisera into the hands of a woman." So Deborah went with Barak to Kedesh. Barak then mustered Zebulun and Naphtali at Kadesh; ten thousand men marched up after him; and Deborah also went up with him.

Now Heber the Kenite had separated from the other Kenites, descendants of Hobab, father-in-law of Moses, and had pitched his tent at Elon-bezaanannim, which is near Kedesh.

Sisera was informed that Barak son of Abinoam had gone up to Mount Tabor. So Sisera ordered all his chariots—nine hundred iron chariots—and all the troops he had to move from Harosheth-goiimm to the Wadi Kishon. Then Deborah said to Barak, "Up! This is the day on which the Lord will deliver Sisera into your hands: the Lord is marching before you." Barak charged down Mount Tabor, followed by the ten thousand men, and the Lord threw Sisera and all his chariots and army into a panic before the onslaught of Barak. Sisera leaped from his chariot and fled on foot as Barak pursued the chariots and the soldiers as far as Harosheth-goiim. All of Sisera's soldiers fell by the sword; not a man was left.

Sisera, meanwhile, had fled on foot to the tent of Jael, wife of Heber the Kenite; for there was friendship between King Jabin of Hazor and the family of Heber the Kenite. Jael came out to greet Sisera and said to him, "Come in, my lord, come in here, do not be afraid." So he entered her tent, and she covered him with a blanket. He said to her, "Please let me have some water; I am thirsty." She opened a skin of milk and gave him some to drink; and she covered him again. He said to her, "Stand at the entrance of the tent. If anybody comes and asks you if there is anybody here, say 'No.'" Then Jael wife of Heber took a tent pin and grasped the mallet. When he was fast asleep from exhaustion, she approached him stealthily and drove the pin through his temple till it went down to the ground. Thus he died.

Now Barak appeared in pursuit of Sisera. Jael went out to greet him and said, "Come, I will show you the man you are looking for." He went inside with her, and there was Sisera lying dead, with the pin in his temple.

On that day God subdued King Jabin of Hazor before the Israelites. The hand of the Israelites bore harder and harder on King Jabin of Canaan, until they destroyed King Jabin of Canaan. On that day Deborah and Barak son of Abinoam sang:

> When locks go untrimmed in Israel,
> When people dedicate themselves—
> Bless the Lord!
>
> Hear, O kings! Give ear, O potentates!
> I will sing, will sing to the Lord,
> Will hymn the Lord, God of Israel.
>
> O Lord, when You came forth from Seir,
> Advanced from the country of Edom,
> The earth trembled;
> The heavens dripped,
> Yea, the clouds dripped water,
> The mountains quaked—
> Before the Lord, Him of Sinai,
> Before the Lord, God of Israel.
>
> In the days of Shagmar son of Anath,
> In the days of Jael, caravans ceased,
> And wayfarers went
> By roundabout paths.
> Deliverance ceased,
> Ceased in Israel,
> Till you arose, O Deborah,
> Arose, O mother, in Israel!
> When they chose new gods,
> Was there a fighter then in the gates?

No shield or spear was seen
Among forty thousand in Israel!

My heart is with Israel's leaders,
With the dedicated of the people—
Bless the Lord!
You riders on tawny she-asses,
You who sit on saddle rugs,
And you wayfarers, declare it!
Louder than the sound of archers,
There among the watering places
Let them chant the gracious acts of the Lord,
His gracious deliverance of Israel.
Then did the people of the Lord
March down to the gates!
Awake, awake, O Deborah!
Awake, awake, strike up the chant!
Arise O Barak;
Take your captives, O son of Abinoam!

Then was the remnant made victor over the mighty,
The Lord's people won my victory over the warriors.

From Ephraim came they whose roots are in Amelek;
After you, your kin Benjamin;
From Machir came down leaders,
From Zebulun such as hold the marshall's staff.
And Issachar's chiefs were with Deborah;
As Barak, so was Issachar—
Rushing after him into the valley.

Among the clans of Reuben
Were great decisions of heart.
Why then did you stay among the sheepfolds
And listen as they pipe for the flocks?
Among the clans of Reuben
Were great searchings of heart!
Gilead tarried beyond the Jordan;
Dan—why did he linger by the ships?

Asher remained at the seacoast
And tarried at his landings.
Zebulun is a people that mocked at death,
Naphtali—on the open heights.

Then the kings came, they fought:
The kings of Canaan fought
At Taanach, by Megiddo's waters—
They got no spoil of silver.
The stars fought from heaven,
From their courses they fought against Sisera,
The torrent Kishon swept them away,
The raging torrent, the torrent Kishon.

March on, my soul, with courage!

Then the horses' hoofs pounded
As headlong galloped the steeds.
"Curse Meroz!" said the angel of the Lord.
"Bitterly curse its inhabitants,
Because they came not to the aid of the Lord,
To the aid of the Lord among the warriors."

Most blessed of women be Jael,
Wife of Heber the Kenite,
Most blessed of women in tents.
He asked for water, she offered milk;
In a princely bowl she brought him curds.
Her [left] hand reached for the tent pin,
Her right for the workmen's hammer.
She struck Sisera, crushed his head,
Smashed and pierced his temple.
At her feet he sank, lay outstretched,
At her feet he sank, lay still;
Where he sank, there he lay—destroyed.

Through the window peered Sisera's mother,
Behind the lattice she whined:

"Why is his chariot so long in coming?
Why so late the clatter of his wheels?"
The wisest of all her ladies give answer;
She, too, replies to herself:
"They must be dividing the spoil they have found:
A damsel or two for each man,
Spoil of dyed cloths for Sisera,
Spoil of embroidered cloths.
A couple of embroidered cloths
Round every neck as spoil."

So may all Your enemies perish, O Lord!
But may His friends be as the sun rising in might!

And the land was tranquil for forty years (Judges 4:1–5:31).

Rabbinic Midrashim

These two midrashim present contrasting views of Deborah and of women as leaders. What message does the first one give? What qualifications for leadership does the second one suggest? To what extent do you think these opposing views are still held, especially with regard to Jewish communal life?

R. Berechiah had four sayings, three concerning men, and one concerning women: Woe unto the living who needs help from the dead. Woe unto the strong who needs help from the weak. Woe unto the seeing who needs help from the blind. Woe unto the generation whose leader is a woman as when DEBORAH, A PROPHETESS . . . JUDGED ISRAEL [Judges 4:4].[1]

NOW DEBORAH, A PROPHETESS, THE WIFE OF LAPPIDOTH, SHE JUDGED ISRAEL AT THAT TIME [Judges 4:4]. What was the

---

1. "The Midrash on Psalms 22:20," in *The Midrash on Psalms*, trans. William G. Braude (New Haven, CT: Yale University Press, 1959).

special character of Deborah that qualified her to prophesy about Israel and to judge them? Was not Phineas son of Eleazar still alive at that time? In the school of Elijah it was taught: I call heaven and earth to witness that whether it be a heathen or a Jew, a man or a woman, a manservant or a maidservant, the holy spirit will suffuse any one of them in keeping with the deeds he or she performs.

[What were Deborah's meritorious deeds?] It is said that Deborah's husband was unlettered [in Torah]. So his wife told him: "Come, I will make wicks for you; take them to the Holy Place in Shiloh. Your portion will then be with men of worth in Israel [who will be studying by the light of your wicks], and you will be worthy of life in the world-to-come." She took care to make the wicks thick, so that their light would be ample. He brought these wicks to the Holy Place [in Shiloh]. The Holy One, who examines the hearts and reins of mankind, said to her: Deborah, since you took care to make the light for the study of my Torah ample, I will make the light of your prophecy ample in the presence of Israel's twelve tribes.[2]

"Awake, Sing!"

by Leila Leah Bronner

"Awake, Sing!" is excerpted from Leila Leah Bronner's book, From Eve to Esther: Rabbinic Reconstructions of Biblical Women. *In it, Bronner demonstrates that the view of Deborah held by the first midrash in this chapter is the predominant one in rabbinic literature. She wonders, "Why did no one give the contrary view?" How would you answer her? How would you portray Deborah?*

2. *Seder Eliyyahu Rabbah*, ed. Meir Friedmann (Vienna, 1902, 1904), p. 48; *Yalkut Shimoni*, Judges 42, in *The Book of Legends*, ed. Hayim Nahman Bialik and Yehoshua Hana Ravnitzky; trans. William G. Braude (New York: Schocken Books, 1992).

Two outstanding women leaders mentioned in the Bible are Deborah
and Huldah. Indeed . . . the rabbis acknowledge them as prophetesses.
But their public careers discomfited the rabbis, who had no such
immediate models and no established methodological principles for
dealing with women of this caliber. Through their treatment of Deborah,
in particular, we can see how they adjusted or altered the reality to meet
their own preconceptions about powerful women. They do this largely
through three approaches: defining her husband, attributing to her the
unlovely quality of hubris (leaders often overstep that border, an
invitation to midrashic transformation), and redefining her functions.

The Bible introduces Deborah as a prophetess who is married to a
man named Lappidoth. Thus the rabbis turn to discover what type of
person Deborah's husband was. Their investigation is more fanciful than
factual, and this type of rabbinic scrutiny concerning a woman's husband
is not found in connection with any other female figure whose husband
is mentioned in scripture. The rabbinic mind tends to define women as
belonging to men, not vice versa. So the Midrash proceeds to discuss
what is meant by the words 'eshet Lappidoth, literally, a "woman of
flames," as well as "the wife of Lappidoth." Some sages said that
Deborah's husband was an ignorant man and that she made wicks for the
Sanctuary on his behalf so that he might achieve merit and gain a share
in the world to come.[3]

Other exegetical sources discuss whether Barak, the leader of the
army, was her husband. If he was her husband, why did she have to send
for him? The Midrash comments on the biblical verses as follows:

> She summoned Barak son of Abinoam, of Kedesh in Naphtali, and said to
> him, "The Lord, the God of Israel, has commanded: 'Go, march up to
> Mount Tabor . . .'" (Judges 4:6–7). What connection was there between
> Deborah and Barak and between Barak and Deborah, since, to begin with,
> they lived some distance from each other; Deborah in her place (Mount
> Ephraim), and Barak in his place (Kedesh in Naphtali)? The answer is that
> Barak ministered to the elders during the life of Joshua and after Joshua

3. b. Megillah 14b; cf. Midrash Eliahu Rabba (Tanna Debe Eliyahu), ch. 9,
edited by M. Friedmann [Ish-Shalom] (1904; reprint, Jerusalem: Wahrman
Books, 1960), pp. 48ff.

continued to minister to them. Therefore it came about that he was fetched and joined in marriage to Deborah (who as an elder in Israel was worthy of his ministering to her).[4]

Kimhi, a medieval exegete, suggested that just as Moses separated himself from his wife when he became a prophet, so Deborah, when she became a prophetess, separated from her husband; therefore they lived apart and she had to send for him.[5] Other sages attempt to show that Barak and Lappidoth were not identical, because Barak was a learned person, unlike the ignorant Lappidoth.

Another midrashic tradition gives Deborah's husband three different names:

> In fact he had three names—Barak, Lappidoth, and Michael: Barak, because his face had the livid look of lightning; Lappidoth, because he used to make wicks which he took to the Holy Place in Shiloh; and Michael, which was his given name.[6]

The names Barak and Lappidoth are explained in this midrashic text, but not Michael, which is elsewhere explained as one who humbles himself.[7] The *Yalqut Shimoni* connects the name with the Hebrew root *mwkh*, translating "he made himself humble and therefore his name is Michael." Or perhaps this midrash is intended as a dig at Deborah, whose husband exhibits humility, a quality that is the reverse of the arrogance attributed to her? The rabbinic connection between Barak and Lappidoth might have emerged from the semantic similarity between the terms *barak* and *lappidoth*, both associated with fire or light.[8]

Now we turn to the unsettling matter of rabbinic tradition attributing arrogance to Deborah. In the words of Rav Nachman, a fourth century Amora:

> Haughtiness does not befit women. There were two haughty [arrogant] women and their names are hateful, one being called a hornet, *ziborata*

---

4. Ibid.
5. David Kimhi (1160?–1235?) on Judges 4:6.
6. *Midrash Eliahu Rabba* 9, in ibid.
7. *Yalqut Shimoni* (Jerusalem: Lewin/Epstein, 1941–1942), Judges 4:1.
8. *Midrash Eliahu Rabba*, ch. 10, p. 50.

(Deborah), and the other a weasel, *kurkushta* (Huldah). Of the hornet it is written, "And she sent and called Barak, instead of going to him." Of the weasel it is written, "Say to the man," instead of "Say to the king."[9]

The larger context in which this passage appears implies that R. Nachman was suggesting that the names (given in the passage in Aramaic) are ugly and are indicative of the personalities of these women. Traditionally, names in the Bible and Talmud are taken very seriously, for they are regarded both as a key to the person named and as a guide to his or her personality. Elijah, for instance, is, according to scholars, called by the name "YHWH is God" to demonstrate that every fiber of his being was devoted to worship.[10] Although the theophoric names {names that include a Divine name} are rare for women in scripture, women are often given animal names without any suggestion that such names are negative—however, not in this midrash.[11]

Deborah's arrogance comes up in another passage, this time from the Talmud.[12] "Rav Judah said in Rav's name: 'Whoever is boastful, if he is a sage, his wisdom departs from him: if he is a prophet, his prophecy departs from him.'" Rabbi Hillel claims that this can be demonstrated from the experience of Deborah, who boasted: "The rulers ceased in Israel, they ceased, until I arose, Deborah, I arose a mother in Israel." Her

---

9. b. *Megillah* 14b.

10. Leila L. Bronner, *The Stories of Elijah and Elisha* (Leiden, Netherlands: E. J. Brill, 1968), p. 23.

11. It is interesting to note that Josephus (Jewish Antiquities 5.5.2 [200]) states that the people sought help from a prophetess whose name was Deborah, which meant "a bee" in Hebrew. Though he attributes no sinister connotations to the name, in light of the later rabbinic comment it is of interest that he mentions it at all. It is amusing to note that Semonides of Amorgos, who lived in the seventh century B.C.E., in his unflattering description of the creation of woman, enumerates seven animals from which woman was made. He claims that only the one made of the bee is a good wife. This early Hellenic tradition had obviously not reached the sages. See further *Encyclopaedia Judaica*, vol. 12 (Jerusalem: Keter Publishing House, 1972), pp. 803ff.; and J. P. Sullivan, *Women in Classical Literature* (Los Angeles: University of California at Los Angeles, 1988), pp. 5–7.

12. b. *Peshaim*, 66a.

words are followed by "Awake, awake, Deborah, awake, awake, utter a song" (Judges 5:12). Rabbinic exegesis explains that because Deborah boasted that she was a mother in Israel she was punished and the Holy Spirit was taken from her. "Awake, utter a song" was taken as an indication that the song had left her. How could the rabbis have faulted her for referring to herself a "a mother in Israel"? The sages do not say how she should have referred to herself and why that statement would merit the loss of prophecy. Clearly, there was more going on than meets the eye.

Deborah's career as judge disturbs the halakhic guidelines of the sages. For one thing, they could not accept a woman in this powerful leadership role. Regarding her role as judge, they discuss the matter at length, and a consensus is reached that she was only a prophetess appointed by God's word, but not a judge. From this interpretation of Deborah as prophetess rather than judge comes the basis for the rabbinic disqualification of women to act as judges.[13] A late midrash, *Tanna Debe Eliyahu*, took a far more liberal stance toward women fulfilling a nontraditional role. Apparently surprised to find Deborah acting as prophetess, leader, and judge, this midrash comments that the spirit of the Lord rests upon individuals according to their deeds and not because of race or gender. The Midrash states:

> What was the special character of Deborah that she, too, judged Israel and prophesied . . . ? In regard to her deeds, I call heaven and earth to witness that whether it be a heathen or a Jew, whether it be a man or a woman, a manservant or a maidservant, the holy spirit will suffuse each of them in keeping with the deeds he or she performs.[14]

The issue of modesty also arises in connection with Deborah's role as judge. . . . [T]he rabbis formulated the law of *yihud*, according to which a man and a woman were not permitted to be alone together in closed quarters, something a judge must do in investigating testimony. To solve the problem of modesty, the rabbis point out that she held court under a palm tree, ensuring that she was not left alone with a man in the course

13. *Tosafot Niddah* 50a.
14. *Midrash Eliahu Rabba*, ch. (9)10, p. 152; cf. Galatians 3:28.

of fulfilling her duties.[15] This model approves of her modestly teaching and counseling outdoors to avoid being secluded with men. As it says in Judges:

> Deborah, wife of Lappidoth, was prophetess; she led Israel at that time. She used to sit under the Palm of Deborah, between Ramah and Bethel in the hill country of Ephraim, and the Israelites would come to her for decisions (Judges 4:4).

Summing up the discussion about Deborah, it is beyond doubt that scripture shows her as a full-fledged prophetess, teaching and leading the people of Israel in a time of crisis. The song attributed by tradition to Deborah (Judges 5) is considered by many scholars as one of the greatest ancient Hebrew poems. Although the rabbis acknowledge Deborah's greatness as prophetess, they had difficulties in coming to terms with the idea of a woman acting as a leader of such stature and authority. By analyzing this great biblical figure in terms of the "unwomanly" trait of arrogance, the rabbis diminish her towering image as a leader. Surprisingly, not one sage comes to her defense or suggests a different interpretation. This is not in keeping with the typical talmudic discussion, in which both pro and con arguments are given. Why did no one give the contrary view that scripture offers no evidence to indicate that she was arrogant?

---

15. b. *Megillah* 14b.

11

JEPHTHAH'S DAUGHTER

Jephthah's Daughter in the Bible

Although the Bible condemns human sacrifice, we find in the Book of Judges the story of the sacrifice of Jephthah's daughter. Why do you think this story is included?

As you read, consider the text's response to Jephthah's vow and his fulfillment of it. Is this what you would expect? What do you make of Jephthah's comments as his daughter ran from the house to meet him? Why do you think she responded as she did? Why does she remain nameless? Should the lost ritual of singing dirges for Jephthah's daughter be restored?

Jephthah the Gileadite was an able warrior, who was the son of a prostitute. Jephthah's father was Gilead; but Gilead also had sons by his wife, and when the wife's sons grew up, they drove Jephthah out. They said to him, "You shall have no share in our father's property, for you are the son of an outsider." So Jephthah fled from his brothers and settled in the Tob country. Men of low character gathered about Jephthah and went out raiding with him.

Some time later, the Ammonites went to war against Israel. And

when the Ammonites attacked Israel, the elders of Gilead went to bring
Jephthah back from the Tob country. They said to Jephthah, "Come be
our chief, so that we can fight the Ammonites." Jephthah replied to the
elders of Gilead, "You are the very people who rejected me and drove me
out of my father's house. How can you come to me now when you are in
trouble?" The elders of Gilead said to Jephthah, "Honestly, we have now
turned back to you. If you come with us and fight the Ammonites, you
shall be our commander over all the inhabitants of Gilead." Jephthah
said to the elders of Gilead "[Very well,] if you bring me back to fight the
Ammonites and the Lord delivers them to me, I am to be your
commander." And the elders of Gilead answered Jephthah, "The Lord
Himself shall be witness between us: we will do just as you have said."

Jephthah went with the elders of Gilead, and the people made him
their commander and chief. And Jephthah repeated all these terms
before the Lord at Mizpah (Judges 11:1–11).

. . . Then the spirit of the Lord came upon Jephthah. He marched
through Gilead and Manasseh, passing Mizpeh of Gilead; and from
Mizpeh of Gilead he crossed over [to] the Ammonites. And Jephthah
made the following vow to the Lord: "If you deliver the Ammonites into
my hands, then whatever comes out of the door of my house to meet me
on my safe return from the Ammonites shall be the Lord's and shall be
offered by me as a burnt offering."

Jephthah crossed over to the Ammonites and attacked them, and the
Lord delivered them into his hands. He utterly routed them—from Aroer
as far as Minnith, twenty towns—all the way to Abel-cheramim. So the
Ammonites submitted to the Israelites.

When Jephthah arrived at his home in Mizpah, there was his daughter
coming out to meet him, with timbrel and dance! She was an only child; he
had no other son or daughter. On seeing her, he rent his clothes and said,
"Alas, daughter! You have brought me low; you have become my troubler!
For I have uttered a vow to the Lord and I cannot retract."

"Father," she said, "you have uttered a vow to the Lord; do to me as
you have vowed, seeing that the Lord has vindicated you against your
enemies, the Ammonites." She further said to her father, "Let this be
done for me: let me be for two months, and I will go with my companions
and lament upon the hills and there bewail my maidenhood." "Go," he
replied. He let her go for two months, and she and her companions went

and bewailed her maidenhood upon the hills. After two months' time, she returned to her father, and he did to her as he had vowed. She had never known a man. So it became a custom in Israel for the maidens of Israel to go every year, for four days in the year, and chant dirges for the daughter of Jephthah the Gileadite (Judges 11:29–40).

Rabbinic Midrash

This midrash argues that Jephthah's vow was improper, and that God answered him in a like manner. Does the idea that God sent Jephthah's daughter out to meet him change your perception of the story? Compare and contrast this account, especially in light of the rabbinic commentary, to the Akedah, the binding and near-sacrifice of Isaac (Genesis 22). Was Jephthah, like Abraham, put to the test? Why did God intervene in the case of Isaac and not in the case of Jephthah's daughter?

Note also that this midrash focuses exclusively on Jephthah's culpability, and virtually ignores the plight of his daughter.

Four people began their supplication by making vows. Three of them made their request in an improper manner and the Holy One, blessed be He, answered them favourably, while one made the request in an improper manner and the Omnipresent answered him correspondingly. They are as follows: Eliezer the servant of Abraham, Saul, Jephthah, and Caleb. Eliezer made his request in an improper manner, as is proved by the text, SO LET IT COME TO PASS, THAT THE DAMSEL TO WHOM I SHALL SAY: LET DOWN THY PITCHER, I PRAY THEE . . . LET THE SAME BE SHE THAT THOU HAST APPOINTED FOR THY SERVANT, EVEN FOR ISAAC (Genesis 24:14). Said the Holy One, blessed be He, to him: "If a Canaanite slave-girl, or a harlot, had come out, would you still have said, LET THE SAME BE SHE THAT THOU HAST APPOINTED FOR THY SERVANT, EVEN FOR ISAAC?" Yet the Holy One, blessed be He, did well for him and brought Rebekah to his hand. Caleb made a request in an improper manner; as it is proved by the text, AND CALEB SAID: HE THAT

SMITETH KIRIATH-SEPHER, AND TAKETH IT, TO HIM WILL I
GIVE ACHSAH MY DAUGHTER TO WIFE (Joshua 15:16). The Holy
One, blessed be He, replied: "If a Canaanite, or a bastard, or a slave had
captured it, would you have given him your daughter?" What, however,
did the Holy One, blessed be He, do? He brought him his brother and the
latter captured it; as it says, AND OTHNIEL THE SON OF KENAZ,
THE BROTHER OF CALEB TOOK IT (ibid., 17). Saul made a request
in an improper manner, as is proved by the text, AND IT SHALL BE,
THAT THE MAN WHO KILLETH HIM, THE KING WILL ENRICH
HIM WITH GREAT RICHES, AND WILL GIVE HIM HIS DAUGH-
TER (1 Samuel 17:25). Said the Holy One, blessed be He, "If an
Ammonite, or a bastard, or a slave had killed him, would you have given
him your daughter?" But the Holy One, blessed be He, brought him
David, and he gave his daughter Michal to him. Jepthah made a request
in an improper manner, as is proved by the text, THEN IT SHALL BE,
THAT WHATSOEVER COMETH FORTH OF THE DOORS OF MY
HOUSE TO MEET ME . . . I WILL OFFER IT UP (Judges 11:31).
Said the Holy One, blessed be He: "If a camel, or an ass, or a dog had
come out, would you have offered it for a burnt-offering?" So the Holy
One, blessed be He, answered him correspondingly by bringing him his
daughter to hand. AND IT CAME TO PASS, WHEN HE SAW HER,
THAT HE RENT HIS CLOTHES (ibid., 35). But surely he could have
had his vow disallowed by going to Phineas? He thought: I am a king!
Shall I go to Phineas? And Phineas argued: I am a High Priest and the
son of a High Priest! Shall I go to that ignoramus? Between the two of
them, the poor maiden perished, and both of them incurred responsibility
for her blood. As regards Phineas, the Holy Spirit departed from him; as
is proved by the text, AND PHINEAS THE SON OF ELEAZAR WAS
RULER OVER THEM, IN TIMES PAST THE LORD WAS WITH
HIM (1 Chronicles 9:20). As regards Jepthah, limb after limb fell off his
body and was buried separately; as is proved by the text, AND WAS
BURIED IN THE CITIES OF GILEAD (Judges 12:7). It does not say IN
THE CITY OF GILEAD, but IN THE CITIES OF. This teaches that
limb after limb fell off his body and he was buried in many places. R.
Simeon b. Lakish and R. Johanan hold different opinions on his case.
Resh Lakish says that he should have given money for her and offered a
sacrifice bought with it upon the altar. R. Johanan says that he need not

have given money, for we have learned: An animal that is fit to be offered on the altar should be offered, while one that is not fit to be offered on the altar should not be offered.[1]

From Texts of Terror
by Phyllis Trible

This excerpt from Phyllis Trible's Texts of Terror *focuses on Jephthah's daughter as "an unmistakable symbol for all the courageous daughters of faithless fathers." Of what other things might she be a symbol? How would you lament her fate?*

~❦~

Like the daughters of Israel, we remember and mourn the daughter of Jephthah the Gileadite. In her death we are all diminished; by our memory she is forever hallowed. Though not a "survivor," she becomes an unmistakable symbol for all the courageous daughters of faithless fathers. Her story, brief as it is, evokes the imagination, calling forth a reader's response. Surely words of lament are a seemly offering, for did not the daughters of Israel mourn the daughter of Jephthah every year? Now the biblical tradition itself provides both a model and foil for just such an offering: the lament of David for Saul and Jonathan, for a father and son who died prematurely in the violence of battle (2 Samuel 1:19–27). Overcome by grief, David cried: "Thy glory, O Israel, is slain upon thy high places!/ How are the mighty fallen!" (2 Samuel 1:19).

Using these haunting words as point and counterpoint, let us in the spirit of the daughters of Israel remember and mourn the daughter of Jephthah:

---

1. *Leviticus Rabbah* 37:4, in *The Midrash*, ed. and trans. H. Freedman and Maurice Simon et al. (London: Soncino Press, 1951).

Thy daughter, O Israel, is slain upon thy high places!
    How are the powerless fallen!
Tell it in Ammon,
    Publish it in the streets of Rabbah;
for the daughters of the Ammonites will not rejoice;
    the daughters of the enemies will not exult.

Tell it also in Gilead,
    publish it in the streets of Mizpah;
for the sons of Israel do forget,
    the sons of the covenant remember not at all.

Ye valleys of Gilead,
    let there be no dew or rain upon you,
    nor upsurging of the deep,
for there the innocence of the powerless was defiled,
    the only daughter of the mighty was offered up.

From the tyranny of the vow,
    from the blood of the sacrifice,
the unnamed child turned not back,
    the courage of the daughter turned not away.

Daughter of Jephthah, beloved and lovely!
    In life and in death a virgin child,
Greeting her father with music and dances,
    facing his blame with clarity and strength.

Ye daughters of Israel, weep for your sister,
    who suffered the betrayal of her foolish father,
    who turned to you for solace and love.

How are the powerless fallen
    in the midst of the victory!

The daughter of Jephthah lies slain upon thy high places.
I weep for you, my little sister.

Very poignant is your story to me;
>your courage to me is wonderful,
>surpassing the courage of men.

How are the powerless fallen,
>a terrible sacrifice to a faithless vow!

12

HANNAH

Hannah in the Bible

Hannah's story has become both prayer and taunt for many infertile women: she agonizes over her barrenness, yet her prayer is ultimately answered.

Like Rachel, Hannah is the beloved wife, childless, and subject to daily intentional and unintentional hurts by fertile co-wives and their children. As you read, compare the way Hannah copes with her infertility to Rachel's actions. In what ways are they similar? How are they different? Why do you think barrenness occurs so frequently among biblical women?

Consider also the way the two men in the narrative respond to Hannah's anguish. What do you think of Elkanah's response? How does Hannah respond to his words?

Hannah is the first average person—male or female—to pray at the Sanctuary, and her plea is misinterpreted. How does she respond to Elkanah's rebuke? Why do you think she chooses to explain herself?

There was a man from Ramathaim of the Zuphites, in the hill country of Ephraim, whose name was Elkanah son of Jeroham son of Elihu son of Tohu son of Zuph, an Ephraimite. He had two wives, one named Hannah and the other Peninnah; Peninnah had children, but Hannah was childless. This man used to go up from his town every year to worship and to offer sacrifice to the Lord of Hosts at Shiloh.--Hophni and Phinehas, the two sons of Eli, were priests of the Lord there.

One such day, Elkanah offered a sacrifice. He used to give portions to his wife Peninnah and to all her sons and daughters; but to Hannah he would give one portion only—though Hannah was his favorite—for the Lord had closed her womb. Moreover, her rival, to make her miserable, would taunt her that the Lord had closed her womb. This happened year after year: Every time she went up to the House of the Lord, the other would taunt her, so that she wept and would not eat. Her husband Elkanah said to her, "Hannah, why are you crying and why aren't you eating? Why are you so sad? Am I not more devoted to you than ten sons?"

After they had eaten and drunk at Shiloh, Hannah rose.—The priest Eli was sitting on the seat near the doorpost of the temple of the Lord.—In her wretchedness, she prayed to the Lord, weeping all the while. And she made this vow: "O Lord of Hosts, if You will look upon the suffering of Your maidservant and will remember me and not forget Your maidservant, and if You will grant Your maidservant a male child, I will dedicate him to the Lord for all the days of his life; and no razor shall ever touch his head."

As she kept on praying before the Lord, Eli watched her mouth. Now Hannah was praying in her heart; only her lips moved, but her voice could not be heard. So Eli thought she was drunk. Eli said to her, "How long will you make a drunken spectacle of yourself? Sober up!" And Hannah replied, "Oh no, my lord! I am a very unhappy woman. I have drunk no wine or other strong drink, but I have been pouring out my heart to the Lord. Do not take your maidservant for a worthless woman; I have only been speaking all this time out of my great anguish and distress." "Then go in peace," said Eli, "and may the God of Israel grant you what you have asked of Him." She answered, "You are most kind to your handmaid." So the woman left, and she ate, and was no longer downcast. Early next morning they bowed low before the Lord, and they went back home to Ramah.

Elkanah knew his wife Hannah and the Lord remembered her. Hannah conceived, and at the turn of the year bore a son. She named him Samuel, meaning "I asked the Lord for him." And when the man

Elkanah and all his household were going up to offer to the Lord the
annual sacrifice and his votive sacrifice, Hannah did not go up. She said
to her husband, "When the child is weaned, I will bring him. For when
he has appeared before the Lord, he must remain there for good." Her
husband Elkanah said to her, "Do as you think best. Stay home until you
have weaned him. May the Lord fulfill His word." So the woman stayed
home and nursed her son until she weaned him.

When she had weaned him, she took him up with her, along with
three bulls, one ephah of flour, and a jar of wine. And though the boy was
still very young, she brought him to the House of the Lord at Shiloh.
After slaughtering the bull, they brought the boy to Eli. She said, "Please,
my lord! As you live, my lord, I am the woman who stood here beside you
and prayed to the Lord. It was this boy I prayed for; and the Lord has
granted me what I asked of Him. I, in turn, hereby lend him to the Lord.
For as long as he lives he is lent to the Lord." And they bowed low there
before the Lord.

And Hannah prayed:

My heart exults in the Lord;
I have triumphed through the Lord.
I gloat over my enemies;
I rejoice in Your deliverance.

There is no holy one like the Lord,
Truly, there is none beside You;
There is no rock like our God.

Talk no more with lofty pride,
Let no arrogance cross your lips!
For the Lord is an all-knowing God;
By Him actions are measured.

The bows of the mighty are broken,
And the faltering are girded with strength.
Men once sated must hire out for bread;
Men once hungry hunger no more.
While the barren woman bears seven,

The mother of many is forlorn.
The Lord deals death and gives life,
Casts down into Sheol and raises up.
The Lord makes poor and makes rich;
He casts down, He also lifts high.
He raises the poor from the dust,
Lifts up the needy from the dunghill,
Setting them with nobles,
Granting them seats of honor.
For the pillars of the earth are the Lord's;
He has set the world upon them.
He guards the steps of His faithful,
But the wicked perish in darkness—
For not by strength shall man prevail.

The foes of the Lord shall be shattered;
He will thunder against them in the heavens.
The Lord will judge the ends of the earth.
He will give power to His king,
And triumph to His anointed one.

Then Elkanah [and Hannah] went home to Ramah; and the boy entered the service of the Lord under the priest Eli (1 Samuel 1:1–2:11).

. . . Samuel was engaged in the service of the Lord as an attendant, girded with a linen ephod. His mother would also make a little robe for him and bring it up to him every year, when she made the pilgrimage with her husband to offer the annual sacrifice. Eli would bless Elkanah and his wife, and say, "May the Lord grant you offspring by this woman in place of the loan she made to the Lord." Then they would return home. For the Lord took note of Hannah; she conceived and bore three sons and two daughters. Young Samuel meanwhile grew up in the service of the Lord (1 Samuel 2:18–21).

Rabbinic Midrashim

Why are the Rabbis so concerned with Peninnah's taunting? As you think about this, remember that polygamy was still legally practiced among Jews in

the period in which this midrash was composed. What do you think of the
explanation as to why Peninnah did this?

What do you think about the plea that the second midrash puts in Hannah's
mouth? Does it sound authentic to you? On what wider issue might it be
commenting?

~❀~

AND HER RIVAL VEXED HER SORE (1 Samuel 1:6). Peninnah would vex Hannah . . . with one annoying taunt after another. What would Peninnah say to her? "Did you get a scarf for your older son and undergarments for your second son?" Then, too, Peninnah would get up early—so said R. Nahman bar Abba—and say to Hannah, "Why don't you rouse yourself and wash your children's faces, so that they will be fit to go to school?" At twelve o'clock, she would say, "Hannah, why don't you rouse yourself and welcome your children who are about to return from school?"

R. Tanhuma bar Abba said: When they sat down to eat, Elkanah would give each of his children his proper portion. Intending to vex Hannah, Peninnah would say to Elkanah, "Give this son of mine his portion and that son of mine his portion. You have given no portion to this [unborn] one." Why did Peninnah speak this way? TO MAKE HER FRET [*hrmh*] (1 Samuel 1:6) against God [for making her barren].

In another comment, the word *hrmh* is interpreted not "to make her fret" but "to make her thunder" against God in prayer on her own behalf. The Holy One said to Peninnah, "You make her 'thunder' against Me. As you live, there are no thunders that are not followed by rain. I shall remember her at once."[1]

NOW HANNAH, SHE SPOKE IN HER HEART {reading "in" as "about"}(1 Samuel 1:13). Eleazar said in the name of R. Jose ben Zimra: she spoke concerning her heart. She said before Him: Sovereign of the

---

1. *Midrash Samuel* 5; *Yalkut*, 1 Samuel 77, in *The Book of Legends*, ed. Hayim Nahman Bialik and Yehoshua Hana Ravnitzky; trans. William G. Braude (New York: Schocken Books, 1992).

Universe, among the things that Thou hast created in woman, Thou hast
not created one without a purpose, eyes to see, ears to hear, a nose to
smell, a mouth to speak, hands to do work, legs to walk with, breasts to
give suck. These breasts that Thou hast put on my heart, are they not to
give suck? Give me a son, so that I may suckle with them.[2]

Hannah and Peninah
by Henny Wenkart

*In this contemporary midrash, Henny Wenkart presents an unusual
understanding of Hannah. What do you think of her interpretation? Do you
like this Hannah? Why do you think she titled the piece "Hannah and Peninah"
rather than just "Hannah"? Does this midrash change the way you understand
the marriages in other biblical narratives, particularly those mentioned here?*

Every Rosh Hashanah we read about the man Elkanah, who had two
wives. Peninah had children, but Hannah had no children. Hannah,
however, was the wife Elkanah loved.

We read this right after reading about our foremother Sarah, another
beloved wife who was barren for a very long time. All the way back to
Adam the men in our stories seem to have needed two women—one to
give them children and assure their continuity, the other to be their best
beloved and exist for them alone, without the distractions of child care.

Adam had the sexy Lilith and then Mother Eve. Abraham's Sarah
finally did give him his son Isaac, but a funny thing—Abraham came
close to killing that son! Isaac was a faithful husband, but *his* son Jacob
actually married sisters, Leah who kept giving him children and barren
Rachel, his true beloved. After long waiting she did have a son, Joseph,
whom Jacob spoiled literally within an inch of his life. She tried to have
another but the birth of Benjamin killed her.

---

2. Babylonian Talmud, *Berakhot* 31b, in *The Babylonian Talmud*, ed. and
trans. I. Epstein et al. (London: Soncino Press, 1935–1952).

So that brings us to Elkanah: His one-liner every year cracks up the female side of the *mechitzah*: "What do you care if you're barren, *Am I not more to you than ten sons?*"

No. But it seems that in Hannah's case her desire for a child was spurred mostly by her rival's taunts: "Go ahead and swing those slim hips of yours in our husband's face—they'll never do what hips are supposed to do. You'll never squeeze out a child through them!" To which Hannah probably replied, "Yes, well yours are two mountains with a tunnel through them. You don't see him spending the rest of the night with you, do you? After you he has to run to me and hold each of my buttocks in the palm of a hand till morning." "Just like any other barren whore," says Peninah.

Little Hannah runs crying to Elkanah, refusing to eat until he comforts her. When he gives gifts to his family, he gives one portion to Peninah and one portion to each of her sons, and a double portion to Hannah. Interesting. This is meant to appease her, as one appeases a jealous child. However, Peninah's portions and those of her sons still total more than Hannah's share. Also, notice that he speaks comfort to Hannah, assures her of his preference, but addresses not one word of rebuke to Peninah, the honored mother of his children.

The central scene of the story takes place during one of the annual festival pilgrimages. Hannah is praying under her breath for a child. Eli, the priest, thinking she is a dissolute and drunken woman, chides her; she says, "Oh no, I'm not the sexy party girl type—I'm the maternal type." Having said this, she is able to conceive the very next time her husband knows her, shows up her rival and also bears a son, and promises to "lend" him to God for the rest of his life while she regains her figure and becomes the undisputed chief wife.

She nurses him a long time. The little toddler tries to play with his older brothers, but she keeps him away from them. Also his Daddy doesn't allow himself to form the bonds of Dad-and-son camaraderie—so soon the child won't be there.

Think about this little boy. He is weaned and has a big party. All the neighbors bring him presents. Soon after, for the first time, he is allowed to go on the pilgrimage with the whole family. In Shiloh he is dazzled by the spectacle, the noise, the music, the animal smells and cries.

At the end of the festival his Mom even introduces him to the great High Priest.

And then she leaves him there.

Think of this little boy. He never goes home with his family again. He stays there with the old man Eli, wanders about, begins to hear voices, and becomes the Prophet Samuel.

13

BATHSHEBA

Bathsheba in the Bible

When she is first introduced, Bathsheba is the daughter of Eliam and the wife of Uriah. King David sees her bathing and, abruptly, she becomes the wife of David and the mother of Solomon. How do you think a woman in such a circumstance might behave—and feel? What does the text tell us about her? Does she come across as a believable character?

How might Bathsheba have felt when the messenger from the king came for her? Was she coerced or did she go by choice? How did she feel when she realized she was pregnant? Was she grief-stricken or relieved when she learned of Uriah's death? How did she cope with the death of her child, which was conceived in sin? How do you think she felt about David?

What details would you add to this narrative? Why do think they have been left out?

~❦~

Late one afternoon, David rose from his couch and strolled on the roof of the royal palace; and from the roof he saw a woman bathing. The woman was very beautiful, and the king sent someone to make inquiries about the woman. He reported, "She is Bathsheba daughter of Eliam

[and] wife of Uriah the Hittite." David sent messengers to fetch her; she came to him and he lay with her—she had just purified herself after her period—and she went back home. The woman conceived, and she sent word to David, "I am pregnant." Thereupon David sent a message to Joab, "Send Uriah the Hittite to me"; and Joab sent Uriah to David.

When Uriah came to him, David asked him how Joab and the troops were faring and how the war was going. Then David said to Uriah, "Go down to your house and bathe your feet." When Uriah left the royal palace, a present from the king followed him. But Uriah slept at the entrance of the royal palace, along with the other officers of his lord, and did not go down to his house. When David was told that Uriah had not gone down to his house, he said to Uriah, "You just came from a journey; why didn't you go down to your house?" Uriah answered David, "The Ark and Israel and Judah are located at Succoth, and my master Joab and your Majesty's men are camped in the open; how can I go home and eat and drink and sleep with my wife? As you live, by your very life, I will not do this!" David said to Uriah, "Stay here today also, and tomorrow I will send you off." So Uriah remained in Jerusalem that day. The next day, David summoned him, and he ate and drank with him until he got him drunk; but in the evening, [Uriah] went out to sleep in the same place, with his lord's officers; he did not go down to his home.

In the morning, David wrote a letter to Joab, which he sent with Uriah. He wrote in the letter as follows: "Place Uriah in the front line where the fighting is fiercest; then fall back so that he may be killed." So when Joab was besieging the city, he stationed Uriah at the point where he knew that there were able warriors. The men of the city sallied out and attacked Joab, and some of David's officers among the troops fell; Uriah the Hittite was among those who died (2 Samuel 11:2–17).

. . . When Uriah's wife heard that her husband Uriah was dead, she lamented over her husband. After the period of mourning was over, David sent and had her brought into his palace; she became his wife and she bore him a son.

But the Lord was displeased with what David had done, and the Lord sent Nathan to David (2 Samuel 11:26–12:1).

. . . David said to Nathan, "I stand guilty before the Lord!" And Nathan replied to David, "The Lord has remitted your sin; you shall not die. However, since you have spurned the enemies of the Lord by this deed, even the child about to be born to you shall die."

Nathan went home, and the Lord afflicted the child that Uriah's wife had borne to David, and it became critically ill. David entreated God for the boy; David fasted, and he went in and spent the night lying on the ground. The senior servants of his household tried to induce him to get up from the ground; but he refused, nor would he partake of food with them. On the seventh day the child died. David's servants were afraid to tell David that the child was dead; for they said, "We spoke to him when the child was alive and he wouldn't listen to us; how can we tell him that the child is dead? He might do something terrible." When David saw his servants talking in whispers, David understood that the child was dead; David asked his servants, "Is the child dead?" "Yes," they replied.

Thereupon David rose from the ground; he bathed and anointed himself, and he changed his clothes. He went into the House of the Lord and prostrated himself. Then he went home and asked for food, which they set before him, and he ate. His courtiers asked him, "Why have you acted in this manner? While the child was alive, you fasted and wept; but now that the child is dead, you rise and take food!" He replied, "While the child was still alive, I fasted and wept because I thought: 'Who knows? The Lord may have pity on me, and the child may live.' But now that he is dead, why should I fast? Can I bring him back again? I shall go to him, but he will never come back to me."

David consoled his wife Bathsheba; he went to her and lay with her. She bore a son and she named him Solomon (2 Samuel 12:13–24).

Rabbinic Midrashim

As in the biblical text, rabbinic midrashim portray Bathsheba as simply David's wife and Solomon's mother. With regard to the former role, she is primarily mentioned in the context of David's sin with her. As Solomon's mother, she is seen as counselor and sometimes disciplinarian, as in this midrash.

Now all Israel were grieved, for it was the day of the dedication of the Temple, and they could not perform the service because Solomon was asleep and they were afraid to wake him, out of their awe of royalty. They went and informed Bathsheba his mother, and she came and woke him up and reproved him. Hence it is written, THE BURDEN WHERE-WITH HIS MOTHER CORRECTED HIM (Proverbs 31:1). R. Joḥanan said: This teaches that his mother bent him over a column and said to him: "WHAT MY SON (ibid., 2)! Everyone knows that your father was a God-fearing man. Now they will speak thus: 'Bathsheba is his mother; she brought him to it!' AND WHAT, O SON OF MY WOMB (ibid.)!"[1]

The Unending Tears of Bat Sheva
by Rabbi Gaylia Rooks

In "The Unending Tears of Bat Sheva," Rabbi Gaylia Rooks puts Bathsheba center-stage. We see her responding to a series of shattering events, culminating in the death of her child. Are her tears for the child or for additional reasons as well?

~🌣~

"And David comforted his wife Bat Sheva and went unto her and lay with her; and she bore a son, and he called his name Solomon" (2 Samuel 12:24).

And when he heard that the child had died, David took off his sackcloth and ashes and washed and annointed himself and he did eat and drink. Then he went to find Bat Sheva.

She sat alone in her garden, rocking back and forth as though with a babe in her arms, yet there was no child for her to suckle at her breast. And when he approached her, she did not turn at his sound and when he sat next to her, she did not glance up.

---

1. *Numbers Rabbah* 10:4, in *The Midrash*, ed. and trans. H. Freedman and Maurice Simon et al. (London: Soncino Press, 1951).

"Bat Sheva. Come my love, my fair one. Rise up and join me in our chambers. Let me comfort you with the warmth of my body and the passion of my soul." "I cannot, David. Not now. Not while he lays yet not cold in the ground."

"My Queen, would that I could spare you this pain. I am King over all Israel, and yet lack the only power I truly desire. My heart is broken twice over. Once at the loss of my son and again at the pain this grief brings to you."

Bat Sheva sat silently. Trying not to blame the King. Knowing in her heart that she loved him still; would love him always. Hating him for the punishment they both must bear for their transgression. Resenting David for his faith and his courage and his willingness to move on with his life. His ability to forge on ahead.

"Bat Sheva, my love, my life. Please. Do not keen over this babe. It tears at my soul." His soul. What does his soul know of my pain? I carried this child for nine months in my womb—our lives intertwined—and now the bond has been so cruelly severed. He is lost from me. Forever. Gone.

And the King arose and gently took Bat Sheva and led her into their chambers and loved her. And as he lay with her, he prayed that a new life might be started that very night to help soothe Bat Sheva's pain.

But as she lay there, silently weeping, she wished only for the comfort of understanding. Why must he ask me not to grieve? How can I not grieve? Can I simply tell my heart to stop its beating? I can't do this again. Not so soon. Not yet. I need time. My body needs time to heal, to forget, and to move on.

Will there ever come an end to the tears? Each time they cease, but a moment passes by and they begin to flow anew. Why does David not cry? It was his child as well. Ill-conceived from his passion whilst I was yet married to Uriah. Why should an infant die for our sins? Does he cry when I cannot see? Will there come a day soon when I can hide my tears, stop the flow until I lie in private? He prays for another son, now. That's so like a man. This one is dead, let us begin right now to start another one. He will find comfort in creating a new life, now with the blessing of marriage. But for me . . . what will comfort me? Will consolation never come? Are there unending tears?

14

RUTH AND NAOMI

Ruth and Naomi in the Bible

Although the Book of Ruth focuses on Ruth and Naomi, it ends with David's genealogy. Some speculate that the book was written as an origin story for the future king. This perspective raises some interesting questions, such as, Why include a convert in the king's line?

Interesting comparisons can be made between Ruth and Tamar. Think especially of their backgrounds and the way in which each of them approached the nearest kinsman to fulfill the obligation of levirite marriage. In fact, the Book of Ruth itself suggests this comparison in verse 4:12: AND MAY YOUR HOUSE BE LIKE THE HOUSE OF PEREZ WHOM TAMAR BORE TO JUDAH. Perez, too, is an ancestor of David.

Also consider the similarities of the relationships of Ruth and Naomi and Jonathan and David. Compare for example, 1 Samuel 18:1, . . . JONATHAN'S SOUL BECAME BOUND UP WITH THE SOUL OF DAVID; JONATHAN LOVED DAVID AS HIMSELF," and Ruth 1:16–17, FOR WHEREVER YOU GO, I WILL GO; WHEREVER YOU LODGE, I WILL LODGE; YOUR PEOPLE SHALL BE MY PEOPLE, AND YOUR GOD MY GOD. WHERE YOU DIE, I WILL DIE, AND THERE I WILL BE BURIED. Some have suggested that these pairs were lovers. What do you think?

Naomi suggests that each of her daughters-in-law return to the house of her mother, as opposed to the (more typical) "house of your father." Why do you think Naomi speaks as she does? Why do you think Orpah chose to return; why did Ruth choose to go on with her mother-in-law?

Naomi changes her name, which means "sweet" or "pleasant," when she returns to Bethlehem, saying, I WENT AWAY FULL AND THE LORD HAS BROUGHT ME BACK EMPTY. How do you think Ruth, standing by her side, felt when she heard this? Do you think Naomi was right to change her name?

~❦~

In the days when the chieftains ruled, there was a famine in the land; and a man of Bethlehem in Judah, with his wife and two sons, went to reside in the country of Moab. The man's name was Elimelech, his wife's name was Naomi, and his two sons were named Mahlon and Chilion—Ephrathites of Bethlehem in Judah. They came to the country of Moab and remained there.

Elimelech, Naomi's husband, died; and she was left with her two sons. They married Moabite women, one named Orpah and the other Ruth, and they lived there about ten years. Then those two—Mahlon and Chilion—also died; so the woman was left without her two sons and without her husband.

She started out with her daughters-in-law to return from the country of Moab; for in the country of Moab she had heard that the Lord had taken note of His people and given them food. Accompanied by her two daughters-in-law, she left the place where she had been living; and they set out on the road back to the land of Judah.

But Naomi said to her two daughters-in-law, "Turn back, each of you to her mother's house. May the Lord deal kindly with you, as you have dealt with the dead and with me! May the Lord grant that each of you find security in the house of a husband!" And she kissed them farewell. They broke into weeping and said to her, "No, we will return with you to your people."

But Naomi replied, "Turn back, my daughters! Why should you go with me? Have I any more sons in my body who might be husbands for you? Turn back, my daughters, for I am too old to be married. Even if I thought there was hope for me, even if I were married tonight and I also bore sons, should you wait for them to grow up? Should you on their account debar yourselves from marriage? Oh no, my daughters! My lot is far more bitter than yours, for the hand of the Lord has struck out against me."

They broke into weeping again, and Orpah kissed her mother-in-law farewell. But Ruth clung to her. So she said, "See, your sister-in-law has returned to her people and her gods. Go follow your sister-in-law." But Ruth replied, "Do not urge me to leave you, to turn back and not follow you. For wherever you go, I will go; wherever you lodge, I will lodge; your people shall be my people, and your God my God. Where you die, I will die, and there I will be buried. Thus and more may the Lord do to me if anything but death parts me from you." When [Naomi] saw how determined she was to go with her, she ceased to argue with her; and the two went on until they reached Bethlehem.

When they arrived in Bethlehem, the whole city buzzed with excitement over them. The women said, "Can this be Naomi?" "Do not call me Naomi," she replied, "Call me Mara, for Shaddai has made my lot very bitter. I went away full, and the Lord has brought me back empty. How can you call me Naomi, when the Lord has dealt harshly with me, when Shaddai has brought misfortune upon me!"

Thus Naomi returned from the country of Moab; she returned with her daughter-in-law Ruth the Moabite. They arrived in Bethlehem at the beginning of the barley harvest.

Now Naomi had a kinsman on her husband's side, a man of substance, of the family of Elimelech, whose name was Boaz.

Ruth the Moabite said to Naomi, "I would like to go to the fields and glean among the ears of grain, behind someone who may show me kindness." "Yes, daughter, go," she replied; and off she went. She came and gleaned in a field, behind the reapers; and, as luck would have it, it was the piece of land belonging to Boaz, who was of Elimelech's family.

Presently Boaz arrived from Bethlehem. He greeted the reapers, "The Lord be with you!" And they responded, "The Lord bless you!" Boaz said to the servant who was in charge of the reapers, "Whose girl is that?" The servant in charge of the reapers replied, "She is a Moabite girl who came back with Naomi from the country of Moab. She said, 'Please let me glean and gather among the sheaves behind the reapers.' She has been on her feet ever since she came this morning. She has rested but little in the hut."

Boaz said to Ruth, "Listen to me, daughter. Don't go to glean in another field. Don't go elsewhere, but stay here close to my girls. Keep your eyes on the field they are reaping, and follow them. I have ordered the men not to molest you. And when you are thirsty, go to the jars and drink some of [the water] that the men have drawn."

She prostrated herself with her face to the ground, and said to him, "Why are you so kind as to single me out, when I am a foreigner?"

Boaz said in reply, "I have been told of all that you did for your mother-in-law after the death of your husband, how you left your father and mother and the land of your birth and came to a people you had not known before. May the Lord reward your deeds. May you have a full recompense from the Lord, the God of Israel, under whose wings you have sought refuge!"

She answered, "You are most kind, my lord, to comfort me and to speak gently to your maidservant—though I am not so much as one of your maidservants."

At mealtime, Boaz said to her, "Come over here and partake of the meal, and dip your morsel in the vinegar." So she sat down beside the reapers. He handed her roasted grain, and she ate her fill and had some left over.

When she got up again to glean, Boaz gave orders to his workers, "You are not only to let her glean among the sheaves, without interference, but you must also pull some [stalks] out of the heaps and leave them for her to glean, and not scold her."

She gleaned in the field until evening. Then she beat out what she had gleaned—it was about an *ephah* of barley—and carried it back to the town. When her mother-in-law saw what she had gleaned, and when she also took out and gave her what she had left over after eating her fill, her mother-in-law asked her, "Where did you glean today? Where did you work? Blessed be he who took such generous notice of you!" So she told her mother-in-law whom she had worked with, saying, "The name of the man with whom I worked today is Boaz."

Naomi said to her daughter-in-law, "Blessed be he of the Lord, who has not failed in His kindness to the living or to the dead! For," Naomi explained to her daughter-in-law, "the man is related to us; he is one of our redeeming kinsmen." Ruth the Moabite said, "He even told me, 'Stay close by my workers until all my harvest is finished.'" And Naomi answered her daughter-in-law Ruth, "It is best, daughter, that you go out with his girls, and not be annoyed in some other field." So she stayed close to the maidservants of Boaz, and gleaned until the barley harvest and the wheat harvest were finished. Then she stayed at home with her mother-in-law.

Naomi, her mother-in-law, said to her, "Daughter, I must seek a home for you, where you may be happy. Now there is our kinsman Boaz, whose girls you were close to. He will be winnowing barley on the threshing floor tonight. So bathe, anoint yourself, dress up, and go down to the threshing floor. But do not disclose yourself to the man until he has finished eating and drinking. When he lies down, note the place where he lies down, and go over and uncover his feet and lie down. He will tell you what you are to do." She replied, "I will do everything you tell me."

She went down to the threshing floor and did just as her mother-in-law had instructed her. Boaz ate and drank, and in a cheerful mood went to lie down beside the grainpile. Then she went over stealthily and uncovered his feet and lay down. In the middle of the night, the man gave a start and pulled back—there was a woman lying at his feet!

"Who are you?" he asked. And she replied, "I am your handmaid Ruth. Spread your robe over your handmaid, for you are a redeeming kinsman."

He exclaimed, "Be blessed of the Lord, daughter! Your latest deed of loyalty is greater than the first, in that you have not turned to younger men, whether poor or rich. And now, daughter, have no fear. I will do in your behalf whatever you ask, for all the elders of my town know what a fine woman you are. But while it is true I am a redeeming kinsman, there is another redeemer closer than I. Stay for the night. Then in the morning, if he will act as a redeemer, good! let him redeem. But if he does not want to act as redeemer for you, I will do so myself, as the Lord lives! Lie down until the morning."

So she lay at his feet until dawn. She rose before one person could distinguish another, for he thought, "Let it not be known that the woman came to the threshing floor." And he said, "Hold out the shawl you are wearing." She held it while he measured out six measures of barley, and he put it on her back.

When she got back to the town, she came to her mother-in-law, who asked, "How is it with you, daughter?" She told her all that the man had done for her; and she added, "He gave me these six measures of barley, saying to me, 'Do not go back to your mother-in-law empty-handed.'" And Naomi said, "Stay here, daughter, till you learn how the matter turns out. For the man will not rest, but will settle the matter today."

Meanwhile, Boaz had gone to the gate and sat down there. And now the redeemer whom Boaz had mentioned passed by. He called, "Come over and sit down here, So-and-so!" And he came over and sat down. Then [Boaz] took ten elders of the town and said, "Be seated here"; and they sat down.

He said to the redeemer, "Naomi, now returned from the country of Moab, must sell the piece of land which belonged to our kinsman Elimelech. I thought I should disclose the matter to you and say: Acquire it in the presence of those seated here and in the presence of the elders of my people. If you are willing to redeem it, redeem! But if you will not redeem, tell me, that I may know. For there is no one to redeem but you, and I come after you." "I am willing to redeem it," he replied. Boaz continued, "When you acquire the property from Naomi and from Ruth the Moabite, you must also acquire the wife of the deceased, so as to perpetuate the name of the deceased upon his estate." The redeemer replied, "Then I cannot redeem it for myself, lest I impair my own estate. You take over my right of redemption, for I am unable to exercise it."

Now this was formerly done in Israel in cases of redemption or exchange: to validate any transaction, one man would take off his sandal and hand it to the other. Such was the practice in Israel. So when the redeemer said to Boaz, "Acquire for yourself," he drew off his sandal. And Boaz said to the elders and to the rest of the people, "You are witnesses today that I am acquiring from Naomi all that belonged to Elimelech and all that belonged to Chilion and Mahlon. I am also acquiring Ruth the Moabite, the wife of Mahlon, as my wife, so as to perpetuate the name of the deceased upon his estate, that the name of the deceased may not disappear from among his kinsmen and from the gate of his home town. You are witnesses today."

All the people at the gate and the elders answered, "We are. May the Lord make the woman who is coming into your house like Rachel and Leah, both of whom built up the House of Israel! Prosper in Ephrathah and perpetuate your name in Bethlehem! And may your house be like the house of Perez whom Tamar bore to Judah—through the offspring which the Lord will give you by this young woman."

So Boaz married Ruth; she became his wife, and he cohabited with her. The Lord let her conceive, and she bore a son. And the women said to Naomi, "Blessed be the Lord, who has not withheld a redeemer from you today! May his name be perpetuated in Israel! He will renew your life and sustain your old age; for he is born of your daughter-in-law, who loves you and is better to you than seven sons."

Naomi took the child and held it to her bosom. She became its foster mother, and the women neighbors gave him a name, saying, "A son is born to Naomi!" They named him Obed; he was the father of Jesse, father of David.

This is the line of Perez; Perez begot Hezron, Hezron begot Ram, Ram begot Amminadab, Amminidab begot Nahshon, Nahshon begot Salmon, Salmon begot Boaz, Boaz begot Obed, Obed begot Jesse, and Jesse begot David (Ruth 1:1–4:22).

Rabbinic Midrashim

With what aspects of Naomi's life are the Rabbis most concerned? How do they perceive a childless widow? What do you think of the ox analogy in the third midrash?

How do the Rabbis understand Ruth's relationship with Naomi? How does it compare to your understanding? Why do you think the Rabbis might have chosen to interpret Ruth's words to Naomi in this way?

For what qualities do the Rabbis praise Ruth? Do you think that the biblical text supports this interpretation? What qualities do you admire in Ruth and in Naomi?

~👁~

AND THE WOMAN WAS LEFT [Ruth 1:5]. R. Ḥanina said: She was left as the remnants of the remnants {of sacrifice, that is, of no value}.[1]

. . . ALL THE CITY WAS ASTIR CONCERNING THEM, AND THE WOMEN SAID: IS THIS NAOMI? [Ruth 1:19]. Is this the one

---

1. *Ruth Rabbah* 2:10, in *The Midrash*, ed. and trans. H. Freedman and Maurice Simon et al. (London: Soncino Press, 1951).

whose actions were fitting and pleasant (*ne'imim*)? In the past, she used to go in a litter, and now she walks barefoot, and you say, IS THIS NAOMI? In the past she wore a cloak of fine wool and now she is clothed in rags, and you say, IS THIS NAOMI? Before her countenance was ruddy from abundance of food and drink, and now it is sickly from hunger, and yet you say, IS THIS NAOMI? And she said to them, CALL ME NOT NAOMI, CALL ME MARAH [Ruth 1:20]. Bar Ḳappara said: "Her case was like that of an ordinary ox which its owner puts up for sale in the marketplace, saying, 'It is excellent for plowing and drives straight furrows.' 'But,' say the bystanders, 'if it is good for plowing, what is the meaning of those weals on its back?' So said Naomi, WHY CALL YE ME NAOMI (pleasant), SEEING THE LORD HATH TESTIFIED AGAINST ME, AND THE ALMIGHTY HATH AFFLICTED ME [Ruth 1:21].[2]

AND RUTH SAID: ENTREAT ME NOT TO LEAVE THEE, AND TO RETURN FROM FOLLOWING AFTER THEE [Ruth 1:16]. . . . I {Ruth} am fully resolved to become converted under any circumstances, but it is better that it should be at your hands than at those of another. When Naomi heard this, she began to unfold to her the laws of conversion, saying: "My daughter, it is not the custom of daughters of Israel to frequent Gentile theatres and circuses," to which she replied, "WHITHER THOU GOEST, I WILL GO" [ibid.]. She continued: "My daughter, it is not the custom of the daughters of Israel to dwell in a house which has no *mezuzah*," to which she responded, "AND WHERE THOU LODGEST, I WILL LODGE" [ibid.]. THY PEOPLE SHALL BE MY PEOPLE [ibid.] refers to the penalties and admonitions [of the Torah] AND THY GOD MY GOD [ibid.] to the other commandments of the Bible.[3]

. . . WHOSE DAMSEL IS THIS? [Ruth 2:5] Did he {Boaz} then not recognize her? The meaning is that when he saw how attractive she was, and how modest her attitude, he began to inquire concerning her. All the

---

2. *Ruth Rabbah* 3:6, in ibid.
3. *Ruth Rabbah* 2:22, in ibid.

other women bend down to gather the ears of corn, but she sits and gathers; all the other women hitch up their skirts, and she keeps hers down; all the other women jest with the reapers, while she is reserved; all the other women gather from between the sheaves, while she gathers from that which is already abandoned.[4]

Words Not Said:
Four Poems after the Book of Ruth
by Kathryn Hellerstein[5]

Kathryn Hellerstein's "Words Not Said: Four Poems after the Book of Ruth" gives voice to the spoken and unspoken thoughts of the three women of the book. With which aspects of their lives is she most concerned?

Compare the third poem, "Naomi: Call Me Bitter" to the third rabbinic midrash, both of which speak to Naomi's name change. How are they similar—and different?

~☙~

These four poems—dramatic monologues and dialogues—were conceived in the interstices of the Book of Ruth. They attempt to give voice to characters at the few moments when the narrator of the book falls silent, juxtaposing actions that do not follow directly one from the other, or to offer an interpretation of what might lie behind a character's words or deeds. Compared to other narratives in the Bible, Ruth is unified and coherent, with well-developed major characters, who speak their minds at crucial the moments in the story, or, better yet, respond to one another forthrightly. For the most part, Ruth plays itself out in a well-lit foreground, rather than in the shadows of what Erich Auerbach calls a backgrounded narrative, like the Binding of Isaac. Unlike Genesis, Ruth

---

4. *Ruth Rabbah* 4:6, in ibid.
5. The author used the Holy Scriptures (Philadelphia: Jewish Publication Society, 1955).

gives us the most crucial exchanges, between Ruth and Naomi or Ruth and Boaz, that help us see the largesse of spirit inherent in these characters' gentle dealings with one another. Still, there are moments in which the characters' inner lives are not explicit, and my poems depart from four of these.

My models for these dramatizations of the biblical characters are the works of two Yiddish poets, Roza Yakubovitsh and Itzik Manger. Manger is famous for his *Khumesh lider*, first published in Warsaw in 1935, which recast the biblical stories in the clothes and countryside of Jewish Eastern Europe; Yakubovitsh's dramatic monologues, in which biblical women speak in voices at once modern and medieval, came out in Warsaw in 1924 and are virtually unknown today.

Naomi: Loss

"And a certain man of Bethlehem in Judah went to sojourn in the field of Moab, he, and his wife, and his two sons. . . . And Mahlon and Chilion died both of them; and the woman was left of her two children and of her husband" (Ruth 1:1–5).

Suddenly, they are not "his sons" but "my sons."
At the edge of this field sprouting green,
far from the parched hills and stubble
we left for the sake of our children,
I grieve. Why did he leave me so soon? The hunger there
would have killed us. What made Elimelech die here,
where we have plenty? Droplets of morning mist
are as bitter as weeds.

We work the fields. We do without
Bethlehem. Days, nights, I forget.
I sleep alone. Eying the neighbors' daughters,
Chilion and Mahlon choose wives, Orpah and Ruth,
who help me plant and cook. Then, like their father,
both sons die. They make widows of new brides.
Tears splash on muddy paths. Again, seedlings push
aside clods. Their leaflets furl

palely in the fog, promising a good crop
this year. I will have no grandchildren.

Ruth and Orpah (Ruth 1:6)

Then she arose with her daughters-in-law, that she might return from the
field of Moab; for she had heard in the field of Moab that the Lord had
remembered His people in giving them bread.

"There's bread again in Bethlehem!"
breathes Orpah, through her own dull ache
toward where Ruth lies—sad, sleeping form.
Ruth stirs, then sits up, wide awake.

"Naomi certainly will go
when she is told." Ruth rubs her eyes,
"Should we go with her?" "Yes, we must!"
Bride-widows, both gasp in surprise

That yet another change will come.
Then Orpah gets up from her bed,
washes her face, begins to pack
her clothes and bracelets with bowed head.

Ruth stands up, stretches. Then she cries,
"Our families! We will never see
our fathers, mothers, sisters, friends!
The Land of Judah is far away."

But Orpah rolls her blankets, sheets,
and pillow up for traveling,
then over her bright, braided hair,
she pulls a scarf, unraveling

black fringes where she'd torn the edge
in mourning, only weeks before.

Reluctantly, Ruth folds her skirts
and underclothes and says no more.

Naomi: "Call me Bitter" (Ruth 1:19–22)

The path grows stonier, the hills are steep
and sheep and goats graze on the prickly brush.
On terraced plots cling olive trees, their leaves
sigh ashy melodies of my return.
I walked this path ten years ago, going up,
away from Bethlehem, whose walls now glisten
where the road dips and branches out, a maze
of what I've lost and what my God has gained.
Ten years ago, I had to leave behind
this starving puzzle of the ways of God.
I was young then. My husband, hungry for
a better life, trudged at my side, our sons
walked, dreaming of their suppers in Moab.
High noon. The sun is strong. It finds my face
although I want to hide how old I am,
how much I've lost. I'm not alone, there's Ruth,
but how can I without my husband, sons,
be coming home? The women peer out from
their market stalls, their courtyard gates, at Ruth
concealed beside me in her foreign veil,
and ask, "Naomi? Is that you?" I spit.
"Do not call me Naomi, pleasant name.
But call me bitter, Marah, for my God
dealt bitterly with me. He emptied me
of all my fullness. I have nothing now."

Ruth to Naomi: After the Threshing (Ruth 3:6–15)

And she went down unto the threshing-floor, and did according to all that
her mother-in-law bade her.

Without understanding them, I followed your words,
hiding in the shadows of the granary
while threshers—men and boys—ate well and drank.
They fell asleep on bales of hay, their sieves
scattered across the piles of the winnowed grain

as careless as the bawdy jokes and songs
they left off, mid-verse, slipping into dreams.
Stone walls absorbed their even breathing and
fresh dust from beaten husks. I held my breath
as Boaz, laughing, a little drunk, yawned, belched,

then lay down by a heap of corn and slept.
As you instructed, I came softly to
that spot, uncovered his feet—their calloused heels,
worn arches in repose—and curled up there.
At midnight, he turned over, brushed his foot

against my scarf, and suddenly sat up.
"Who are you?" his words probed into the dark.
To him, the rough-edged shadow, darkness on
pure dark, not knowing why, I answered, "Ruth,
your handmaid. Spread your skirt upon me—you

are a near kinsman." His reply blessed me
as "daughter." He praised me for kindness shown
to you, Naomi, and to him, old man
whose grace you ask through me. I never thought
to follow after young men, rich or poor,

or any man, since Mahlon, for when
I followed you, I found my way through grief.
He called me "daughter" again, and "virtuous." His beard
tickled my ear. I shivered in the warmth
of this man's breath, as he explained your laws

that let the nearer kinsman of the dead
be first to choose the widow and the land.

I started to stand up. He told me, "Sleep,"
and just before the dawn broke, helped me leave,
unnoticed, as the moon slipped from a sky—

indigo turned violet—and the sun
inched up to gild the rooftops brilliant as
the barley he poured in my heavy cape.
You ask me, "Daughter, who are you?" I'm filled
with dreams. The chaff of widow falls away.

15

Vashti and Esther

Vashti and Esther in the Bible

The Book of Esther is one of the most fascinating books of the Bible. Many suggest that it be read as a satire, pointing to some of the more fantastic elements of the story such as the year that the virgins spend in preparation for their nights with the king, the ridiculous height of the stake (same say gallows) that Haman builds for Mordecai, and the bountiful references to drinking. In fact, half of all of the references to drinking in the Bible are found in this book. Moreover, there is no mention whatsoever of God.

The text is unclear as to what the king summoned Vashti to do. Tradition holds that she was to dance naked before the king's dinner guests. Modern scholarship suggests that she may have been called to an after-dinner orgy, as if she were a concubine and not a queen. As you read, think about the way in which Vashti is usually portrayed on Purim, the holiday on which the Book of Esther is read. Does that image correspond to the woman presented in the text? Think also about the court's reaction to her disobedience. What does this tell you about the king?

Consider also Esther and the way in which she is usually portrayed. As you read, look for clues to her relationship to her people. What name does she use? Does she observe the dietary laws? Why doesn't she reveal her identity? What does she do when she learns that Mordecai is wearing sackcloth and ashes? How *does she respond to his demand that she come to the aid of her people? Does this close reading change your view of Esther or reinforce it?*

It happened in the days of Ahasuerus—that Ahasuerus who reigned over a hundred and twenty-seven provinces from India to Ethiopia. In those days, when King Ahasuerus occupied the royal throne in the fortress Shushan, in the third year of his reign, he gave a banquet for all the officials and courtiers—the administration of Persia and Media, the nobles and the governors of the provinces in his service. For no fewer than a hundred and eighty days he displayed the vast riches of his kingdom and the splendid glory of his majesty. At the end of this period, the king gave a banquet for seven days in the court of the king's palace garden for all the people who lived in the fortress Shushan, high and low alike. [There were hangings of] white cotton and blue wool, caught up by cords of fine linen and purple wool to silver rods and alabaster columns; and there were couches of gold and silver on a pavement of marble, alabaster, mother-of-pearl, and mosaics. Royal wine was served in abundance, as befits a king, in golden beakers, beakers of varied design. And the rule for the drinking was, "No restrictions!" For the king had given orders to every palace steward to comply with each man's wishes. In addition, Queen Vashti gave a banquet for women, in the royal palace of King Ahasuerus.

On the seventh day, when the king was merry with wine, he ordered Mehuman, Bizzetha, Harbona, Bigtha, Abagtha, Zethar, and Carcas, the seven eunuchs in attendance on King Ahasuerus, to bring Queen Vashti before the king wearing a royal diadem, to display her beauty to the peoples and the officials; for she was a beautiful woman. But Queen Vashti refused to come at the king's command conveyed by the eunuchs. The king was greatly incensed, and his fury burned within him.

Then the king consulted the sages learned in procedure. (For it was the royal practice [to turn] to all who were versed in law and precedent. His closest advisers were Carshena, Shethar, Admatha, Tarshish, Meres, Marsena, and Memucan, the seven ministers of Persia and Media who had access to the royal presence and occupied the first place in the kingdom.) "What," [he asked,] "shall be done, according to law, to Queen

Vashti for failing to obey the command of King Ahasuerus conveyed by the eunuchs?"

Thereupon Memucan declared in the presence of the king and the ministers: "Queen Vashti has committed an offense not only against Your Majesty but also against all the officials and against all the peoples in all the provinces of King Ahasuerus. For the queen's behavior will make all wives despise their husbands, as they reflect that King Ahasuerus himself ordered Queen Vashti to be brought before him, but she would not come. This very day the ladies of Persia and Media, who have heard of the queen's behavior, will cite it to all Your Majesty's officials, and there will be no end of scorn and provocation!

"If it please Your Majesty, let a royal edict be issued by you, and let it be written into the laws of Persia and Media, so that it cannot be abrogated, that Vashti shall never enter the presence of King Ahasuerus. And let Your Majesty bestow her royal state upon another who is more worthy than she. Then will the judgment executed by Your Majesty resound throughout your realm, vast though it is; and all wives will treat their husbands with respect, high and low alike."

The proposal was approved by the king and the ministers, and the king did as Memucan proposed. Dispatches were sent to all the provinces of the king, to every province in its own script and to every nation in its own language, that every man should wield authority in his home and speak the language of his own people.

Some time afterward, when the anger of King Ahasuerus subsided, he thought of Vashti and what she had done and what had been decreed against her. The king's servants who attended him said, "Let beautiful young virgins be sought out for Your Majesty. Let Your Majesty appoint officers in every province of your realm to assemble all the beautiful young virgins at the fortress Shushan, in the harem under the supervision of Hege, the king's eunuch, guardian of the women. Let them be provided with their cosmetics. And let the maiden who pleases Your Majesty be queen instead of Vashti." The proposal pleased the king, and he acted upon it.

In the fortress Shushan lived a Jew by the name of Mordecai, son of Jair son of Shimei son of Kish, a Benjaminite. [Kish] had been exiled from Jerusalem in the group that was carried into exile along with King Jeconiah of Judah, which had been driven into exile by King Nebuchadnezzar of Babylon.—He was foster father to Hadassah—that is, Esther—his uncle's daughter, for she had neither father nor mother. The maiden was shapely and beautiful; and when her father and mother died, Mordecai adopted her as his own daughter.

When the king's order and edict was proclaimed, and when many girls were assembled in the fortress Shushan under the supervision of Hegai, Esther too was taken into the king's palace under the supervision of Hegai, guardian of the women. The girl pleased him and won his favor, and he hastened to furnish her with her cosmetics and her rations, as well as with the seven maids who were her due from the king's palace; and he treated her and her maids with special kindness in the harem. Esther did not reveal her people or her kindred, for Mordecai had told her not to reveal it. Every single day Mordecai would walk about in front of the court of the harem, to learn how Esther was faring and what was happening to her.

When each girl's turn came to go to King Ahasuerus at the end of the twelve month's treatment prescribed for women (for that was the period spent on beautifying them: six months with oil of myrrh and six months with perfumes and women's cosmetics, and it was after that that the girl would go to the king), whatever she asked for would be given her to take with her from the harem to the king's palace. She would go in the evening and leave in the morning for a second harem in charge of Shaashgaz, the king's eunuch, guardian of the concubines. She would not go again to the king unless the king wanted her, when she would be summoned by name. When the turn came for Esther daughter of Abihail—the uncle of Mordecai, who had adopted her as his own daughter—to go to the king, she did not ask for anything but what Hegai, the king's eunuch, guardian of the women, advised. Yet Esther won the admiration of all who saw her.

Esther was taken to King Ahasuerus, in his royal palace, in the tenth month, which is the month of Tebeth, in the seventh year of his reign. The king loved Esther more than all the other women, and she won his grace and favor more than all the virgins. So he set a royal diadem on her head and made her queen instead of Vashti. The king gave a great banquet for all his officials and courtiers, "the banquet of Esther." He proclaimed a remission of taxes for the provinces and distributed gifts as befits a king.

When the virgins were assembled a second time, Mordecai sat in the palace gate. But Esther still did not reveal her kindred or her people, as Mordecai had instructed her; for Esther obeyed Mordecai's bidding, as she had done when she was under his tutelage (Esther 1:1–2:20).

. . . {Haman connives to have all of the Jews in the kingdom executed.} When Mordecai learned all that had happened, Mordecai tore his clothes and put on sackcloth and ashes. He went through the city, crying out loud and bitterly, until he came in front of the palace gate; for one could not enter the palace gate wearing sackcloth.—Also, in every province that the king's command and decree reached, there was great mourning among the Jews, with fasting, weeping, and wailing, and everybody lay in sackcloth and ashes.—When Esther's maidens and eunuchs came and informed her, the queen was greatly agitated. She sent clothing for Mordecai to wear, so that he might take off his sackcloth; but he refused. Thereupon Esther summoned Hathach, one of the eunuchs whom the king had appointed to serve her, and sent him to Mordecai to learn the why and wherefore of it all. Hathach went out to Mordecai in the city square in front of the palace gate; and Mordecai told him all that had happened to him, and all about the money that Haman had offered to pay into the royal treasury for the destruction of the Jews. He also gave him the written text of the law that had been proclaimed in Shushan for their destruction. [He bade him] show it to Esther and inform her, and charge her to go to the king and to appeal to him and to plead with him for her people. When Hathach came and delivered Mordecai's message to Esther, Esther told Hathach to take back to Mordecai the following reply: "All the king's courtiers and the people of the king's provinces know that if any person, man or woman, enters the king's presence in the inner court without having been summoned, there is but one law for him— that he be put to death. Only if the king extends the golden scepter to him may he live. Now I have not been summoned to visit the king for the last thirty days."

When Mordecai was told what Esther had said, Mordecai had this message delivered to Esther: "Do not imagine that you, of all the Jews, will escape with your life by being in the king's palace. On the contrary, if you keep silent in this crisis, relief and deliverance will come to the Jews from another quarter, while you and your father's house will perish. And who knows, perhaps you have attained to royal position for just such a crisis." Then Esther sent back this answer to Mordecai: "Go, assemble all the Jews who live in Shushan, and fast in my behalf; do not eat or drink for three days, night or day. I and my maidens will observe the same fast. Then I shall go to the king, though it is contrary to the law; and if I am to perish, I shall perish!" So Mordecai went about [the city] and did just as Esther had commanded him.

On the third day, Esther put on royal apparel and stood in the inner court of the king's palace, facing the king's palace, while the king was sitting on his royal throne in the throne room facing the entrance of the palace. As soon as the king saw Queen Esther standing in the court, she won his favor. The king extended to Esther the golden scepter which he had in his hand, and Esther approached and touched the tip of the scepter. "What troubles you, Queen Esther?" the king asked her. "And what is your request? Even to half the kingdom, it shall be granted you." "If it please Your Majesty," Esther repled, "let Your Majesty and Haman come today to the feast that I have prepared for him." The king commanded, "Tell Haman to hurry and do Esther's bidding." So the king and Haman came to the feast that Esther had prepared.

At the wine feast, the king asked Esther, "What is your wish? It shall be granted you. And what is your request? Even to half the kingdom, it shall be fulfilled." "My wish," replied Esther, "my request—if Your Majesty will do me the favor, if it please Your Majesty to grant my wish and accede to my request—let Your Majesty and Haman come to the feast which I will prepare for them; and tomorrow I will do your Majesty's bidding" (Esther 4:1–5:8).

. . . So the king and Haman came to feast with Queen Esther. On the second day, the king again asked Esther at the wine feast, "What is your wish, Queen Esther? It shall be granted you. And what is your request? Even to half the kingdom, it shall be fulfilled." Queen Esther replied: "If Your Majesty will do me the favor, and if it pleases Your Majesty, let my life be granted me as my wish, and my people as my request. For we have been sold, my people and I, to be destroyed, massacred, and exterminated. Had we only been sold as bondmen and bondwomen, I would have kept silent; for the adversary is not worthy of the king's trouble."

Thereupon, King Ahasuerus demanded of Queen Esther, "Who is he and where is he who dared to do this?" "The adversary and enemy," replied Esther, "is this evil Haman!" And Haman cringed in terror before the king and the queen. The king, in his fury, left the wine feast for the palace garden, while Haman remained to plead with Queen Esther for his life; for he saw that the king had resolved to destroy him. When the king returned from the palace garden to the banquet room, Haman was lying prostrate on the couch on which Esther reclined. "Does he mean," cried the king, "to ravish the queen in my own palace?" No sooner did these words leave the king's lips than Haman's face was covered. Then Harbonah, one of the eunuchs in attendance on the king, said, "What is more, a stake is standing at Haman's house, fifty cubits high, which Haman made for Mordecai—the man whose words saved the king." "Impale him on it!" the king ordered. So they impaled Haman on the stake which he had put up for Mordecai, and the king's fury abated.

That very day King Ahasuerus gave the property of Haman, the enemy of the Jews, to Queen Esther. Mordecai presented himself to the king, for Esther had revealed how he was related to her. The king slipped off his ring, which he had taken back from Haman, and gave it to Mordecai; and Esther put Mordecai in charge of Haman's property.

Esther spoke to the king again, falling at his feet and weeping, and beseeching him to avert the evil plotted by Haman the Agagite against the Jews. The king extended the golden scepter to Esther, and Esther arose and stood before the king. "If it please Your Majesty," she said, "and if I have won your favor and the proposal seems right to Your Majesty, and if I am pleasing to you—let dispatches be written countermanding those which were written by Haman son of Hammadatha the Agagite, embodying his plot to annihilate the Jews throughout the king's provinces. For how can I bear to see the disaster which will befall my people! And how can I bear to see the destruction of my kindred!"

Then King Ahasuerus said to Queen Esther and Mordecai the Jew, "I have given Haman's property to Esther, and he has been impaled on the stake for scheming against the Jews. And you may further write with regard to the Jews as you see fit. [Write it] in the king's name and seal it with the king's signet, for an edict that has been written in the king's name and sealed with the king's signet may not be revoked" (Esther 7:1–8:8).

Rabbinic Midrashim

What problem seems to concern the Rabbis with regard to Vashti? Why do you think they focus on this issue? How do they view Ahasuerus' treatment of Vashti? How does the rabbinic view of Vashti compare to your own?

How do the Rabbis view Esther? What element do they add to the story that is missing from the biblical text? How does that addition influence your perception of Esther?

Compare the biblical account of Esther's visit to the throne room to that in the last midrash. Do you find any evidence supporting the midrash's view in the Book of Esther? Why do you think the Rabbis created this story?

TO BRING VASHTI THE QUEEN BEFORE THE KING WITH THE CROWN ROYAL (Esther 1:11) . . . when the other nations eat and drink, they turn to lewdness. So here, one said, "The Median women are more beautiful," and the other said, "The Persian women are more beautiful." Said that fool {Ahasuerus} to them: "The vessel which I use is neither Median nor Persian, but Chaldean. Would you like to see it?" They replied, "Yes, but she must be naked." "Very well," he said to them, "let her be naked." R. Phinehas and R. Ḥama b. Guria in the name of Rab said: She asked permission to wear at least as much as a girdle, like a harlot, but they would not allow her. He said to her: "It must be naked." She said, "I will come in without a crown." [He said]: "If so, they will say, 'She is a maidservant.'" Then she [a maidservant] might put on royal garments and enter? R. Huna said: A subject must not put on royal garments.[1]

BUT THE QUEEN VASHTI REFUSED (Esther 1:12). She remonstrated with him very forcibly, saying: "If they consider me beautiful, they will want to enjoy me themselves and kill you; and if they consider me plain, I shall bring disgrace on you." But he was blind to her hints and

---

1. *Esther Rabbah* 3:13, in *The Midrash*, ed. and trans. H. Freeman and Maurice Simon et al. (London: Soncino Press, 1951).

insensible to her pricks. She then sent word to him: "You used to be the stable-boy of my father's house, and you were used to bringing in before yourself naked harlots, and now that you have ascended the throne you have not abandoned your evil habits." He was still blind to her hints and insensible to her pricks. She then sent word to him: "Even those condemned by my father's house were not punished naked," as it says, THEN THESE MEN WERE BOUND IN THEIR CLOAKS, THEIR TUNICS, ETC. (Daniel 3:21).[2]

AND THE QUEEN VASHTI REFUSED (Esther 1:12). Let us see. She was immodest, as the Master said above, that both of them [Vashti and Ahasuerus] had an immoral purpose. Why then would she not come?—

R. Jose b. Hanina said: This teaches that leprosy broke out on her. . . . [I]t was [also] taught that Gabriel came and fixed a tail on her.[3]

AND HE BROUGHT UP HADASSAH (Esther 2:7). Just as the myrtle (*hadassah*) has a sweet smell but a bitter taste, so Esther was sweet to Mordecai but bitter to Haman.[4]

. . . Esther means "the hidden one" for she remained hidden fast in her chambers; but she came forth into the world when there was need of her to give light to Israel.[5]

. . . [A]t that time Esther came into the king's house without permission, as is said ESTHER . . . STOOD IN THE INNER COURT OF THE KING'S HOUSE (Esther 5:1). The king had seven courts: Esther went through the first court, the second, and the third. But as she came into the fourth court, Ahasuerus began gnashing his teeth and

---

2. *Esther Rabbah* 3:14, in ibid.

3. Babylonian Talmud, *Megillah* 12b, in *The Babylonian Talmud*, ed. and trans. I. Epstein et al. (London: Soncino Press, 1935–1952).

4. *Esther Rabbah* 6:5, in *The Midrash*, ed. and trans. H. Freedman and Maurice Simon et al. (London: Soncino Press, 1951).

5. "The Midrash on Psalms 22:3," in *The Midrash on Psalms*, trans. William G. Braude (New Haven, CT: Yale University Press, 1959).

grinding them in rage, and said: "Oh, for those who are gone and cannot be replaced! How I entreated and besought the queen Vashti that she come into my presence! And because she would not come, as it is said BUT THE QUEEN VASHTI REFUSED TO COME (Esther 1:12), I decreed death for her. But this one comes like a harlot without permission!"[6]

NOW IT CAME TO PASS ON THE THIRD DAY, THAT ESTHER PUT ON (Esther 5:1) her most beautiful robes and her richest ornaments, and she took with her two maidens, placing her right hand on one of them and leaning on her, as is the royal custom, while the second maiden followed her mistress bearing her train so that the gold on it should not touch the ground. She put on a smiling face, concealing the anxiety in her heart. Then she came to the inner court facing the king and she stood before him. The king was sitting on his royal throne in a robe adorned with gold and precious stones, and when he lifted up his eyes and saw Esther standing in front of him he was furiously angry because she had broken his law and had come before him without being called. Then Esther lifted up her eyes and saw the king's face, and behold his eyes were flashing like fire with the wrath which was in his heart. And when the queen perceived how angry the king was, she was overcome and her heart sank and she placed her head on the maiden who was supporting her right hand. But our God saw and had mercy on His people, and He took note of the distress of the orphan who trusted in Him and He gave her grace in the eyes of the king and invested her with new beauty and new charm. Then the king rose in haste from his throne and ran to Esther and embraced her and kissed her and flung his arm around her neck and said to her: "Esther, my queen, why dost thou tremble? For this law which we have laid down does not apply to thee, since thou art my beloved and my companion." He also said to her: "Why when I saw you did you not speak to me?" Esther replied: "My lord the king, when I beheld you I was overcome by your high dignity."[7]

---

6. "The Midrash on Psalms 22:24," in ibid.

7. *Esther Rabbah* 9:1, in *The Midrash*, ed. and trans. H. Freedman and Maurice Simon et al. (London: Soncino Press, 1951).

Vashti and the Angel Gabriel

by Jill Hammer

Jill Hammer introduces her tale this way: "I have always been enchanted by the legend that it was the angel Gabriel who convinced Vashti not to go before the king. I wrote this story as a synthesis of many legends about biblical women, and about Gabriel, the angel of strength, and also as an explanation for why there is no Divine Name in the Book of Esther." How does "Vashti and the Angel Gabriel" influence your understanding of Vashti? Is this story consistent with the biblical and rabbinic portrayals of her? Is her view of Esther derived from biblical or rabbinic sources?

~❀~

I could not tell you now the color of his eyes, nor the length of his hair, although he seemed a man to me then. With men I was always observant of such things, for men's vanities were useful in devising flattery and misdirections of all kinds, but in that hour, my eyes learned to see some inner thing, with neither hair nor eyes. With Gabriel, I learned beauty of face, beauty of speech, meant nothing. I learned, also, that in an hour everything can change.

Beauty had meant a great deal to my father, who was a Persian nobleman of impeccable taste. I was his prize ornament. When I was a simpering child, my father brought me sweets and praised my lovely face and graceful form. As I grew, he brought me jewels and praised my beauty still more. Of that within me that was simply Vashti, he was unaware. This was painful but commonplace. Had I been an adult, I would not have minded so much, and would have been grateful for my beauty, which won me privilege and indulgence. As things were, it took me too long to learn to manipulate him, for by the time I was seventeen he had become fixated on the idea of marrying me to the king Ahasuerus, ruler of all Persia, who had recently lost his frail queen. I could remember her crown and her dress but not her face, and the idea of being faceless terrified me. Unfortunately, my sisters were not sufficiently attractive to divert his attention.

Indulged as I was, the simple fact was that my father owned me, and after some coercion on his part I appeared at court. It was not long before the king owned me, and while my wedding night, and many subsequent nights, were unpleasant, at least I had the satisfaction of outranking my father. He made the attempt to advise me from afar, but now I had other advisors, and the king, his time occupied by concubines, hindered me far less than my father had. A woman must get used to anything, and, I often told myself, my lot was better than almost any other woman's, for I needed to neither labor nor starve.

Perhaps, being a bird in a gilded cage, I admired the gilding for too long, not perceiving it for what it was. As queen of the land and mistress of the household, my whims were answered as long as the king took no notice, so I grew adept at escaping his notice. In Shushan, vanity was a survival skill, and I possessed it in plenty. When feasts and celebrations were announced, I paid little or no attention, beyond my contemplation of the young noblemen who might ease my boredom. Imagining the uses of the flesh filled my days, for the spirit that had been nurtured in me was the spirit of flesh, hungry and never satisfied. I became devious and cunning, seeking ways to indulge myself and to outdo in majesty and popularity the king's concubines and the wives of the powerful. I was unhappy, as all are who feel love neither for themselves nor for others, and I blotted out my unhappiness in wine, pleasure, and what mean power was allotted me. And so I passed the years.

In all that time I only engaged in one worthwhile pursuit. I spent my private hours studying books, satisfying a passion all but denied me as a child. In the books I found descriptions of many other worlds, some fanciful, and some entirely beyond my comprehension. I absorbed what I could and ignored what I did not understand. I read tales of romance and epics of the gods, stories of war and histories of ancient Persia. I read the legends of the Jews, their prophets and invisible God, but these were alien to me, for in them was little that I could touch. I was always grasping for substance, beautiful images to fill my eyes and my mind. The tomes I pored over held my attention because I believed that arcane knowledge would gain me more influence, but even when I saw that my influence had not increased, I continued to read. The books were solace for some wound I could not name.

Many hours among those I spent in the palace I do not remember, but this one I remember, for during that hour my fate was rewritten. Having been given permission from the king to hold my own banquet for the noblewomen on his chosen feast day, I was as merry and haughty as a spoiled child, impressing the wives of the ministers with my exquisite gown, with the elaborate ornamentation, the succulent food, the glamour and style of each detail. I was glorying in the murmurs raised by the exquisite dessert when the messenger arrived.

When I understood the summons from the king, I was shocked. It must have been shock, for nothing but shock would have upset my composure in front of my competitors and opponents, the other ladies of the court. Walking, and then running, from the room, I dashed along the corridors until I could no longer hear the voice of the king's herald demanding my answer. I sought a place where my maids in waiting would not think of looking for me.

I happened upon a small, earth-colored chamber looking out on the lush gardens. It held nothing but pots, vases, and flowers. I realized that it must be the room where the servants arranged the palace flowers every day, but I had never seen it before. I gazed upon the fresh, new rosebuds with envy: none could pry them open before their time.

I must have possessed some inherent modesty of which I was unaware, because without it I could not have been so angry. The demand of the king was that I appear nude before his gathered guests, all men, wearing nothing but my crown, in order to prove my superior beauty to his assembled minions. It was a direct order, and I had never defied a direct order. To do so would have been futile, as the king was powerful and I was not, and to anger him would only have weakened my position as queen. I did not consider that I should refuse him now. He was the king; he had the right to command, even when he was drunk and obscene. Yet my skin crawled with rage. Perhaps—since in my vanity I often had imagined the effects of my desirability on hordes of men—it was not modesty that caused my rage but my sense of the unfairness of my position. The king need never accede to the smallest request on my part, and yet I must degrade myself if he wished. The entire court would be reminded that I was the king's chattel, no less than the most forgotten concubine. This day would live in my nightmares.

I attempted to be philosophical—at least the king would protect me from any drunkard who sought to abuse me. His protection was not out of concern for me but for his reputation, yet I was grateful. I plucked a rose from a vase and sniffed it, squeezing my eyes shut, trying to regain my composure, yet when I opened my eyes I had crushed the blossom in my fingers.

A young man rested his elbow against a wide-lipped urn, watching me. In his belt were tucked a scroll and a sheathed weapon. I drew up angrily, imagining that another herald had dared to invade my privacy, but then I sighed, resigned. It seemed that my privacy was not guaranteed, so my indignation on its behalf was foolish. Also, I did not quite want the unfamiliar man to leave. His form, features, and garments were lovely, but it was not that—it was his presence that was beautiful. Perhaps I should have known what he was.

"Do you, too, come to shame a queen?" I inquired icily.

"I have not come to a queen but simply to Vashti," he said gently, surrendering the bright sunshine, which cast its golden light over the urn and slowly approaching me.

Had I been deposed? Or was he one of the pleasing young gentlemen who had noticed my roving eye and become too bold? My curiosity increased, but also my irritation. "Which Vashti is that?" I rapped out sharply, hoping to remind him that my title as queen superseded my identity as an individual, and that if he came to be insolent, he was talking to the wrong woman.

"The Vashti who paces the gardens in the evening and reads books late into the night. The Vashti who feeds herself sweets, gowns, and treasures to satisfy her hunger. The Vashti who keeps her father's gifts hidden away as a remembrance of childhood," he replied. His voice was like a waterfall heard from far away: peaceful, yet commanding attention.

Any man who knew—who noticed—this much about my lifestyle was interesting, and, perhaps, dangerous. Men had often found my directness disarming. I decided that this young blade needed disarming.

"Who are you, and for what reason have you approached me?" I demanded.

"I, Gabriel, have come to plead with you to commit an act of sacred rebellion." The youth spoke with extraordinary self-possession in spite of his strange words. His eyes glowed softly, full of strength. I became afraid of him, and strove not to show my discomfort.

"Rebellion?" I laughed derisively. "Are you an assassin or merely a failed diplomat?"

"I am a messenger. A messenger of God."

"Which god?" Religious fanaticism sustained many at the palace, but it did not interest me in the slightest, as it often seemed to conceal a futile lust for power. I prided myself on good judgement, and I sincerely hoped my curiosity had not been captured so easily by a pious maniac.

"The God who was revealed upon Mount Sinai." Still the expression on the lovely face did not change.

I had read of the beliefs of the Jews, and they sometimes did business at court. At another time, this man's joke or delusion might have amused me, but today, on the day of my impending disgrace, his claim enraged me.

"Have you nothing better to do than mock me with your god!" Once I allowed myself to feel, my emotions of helplessness and fury became uncontrollable. I vented my queenly anger on everything in the room, smashing crystal vases I vaguely remembered having seen in the dining hall. I gathered up flowers and tore at them in my fury, scattering petals, leaves, and fine grains of pollen everywhere.

Gabriel bent and with great care picked up each one of the torn blossoms. As he handled them, they returned to their original whole, beautiful state. They were even more beautiful, their colors more rich, for having been repaired. He is a magician, I thought, but then he himself blossomed and became more beautiful, filled from within with a pure light I could barely manage to look at without blinding myself. He was an angel; I had read about them late at night, almost believing. He was far more than I could have imagined. I knelt on the floor, more from distress than from humility, but he took my hand and helped me to my feet. The light he held within seemed to adjust to my eyes' need, and his voice although strong, held music.

He said to me: "Vashti, be comforted. Your soul is torn, but it will be mended. Your body is enslaved, but you will be free, for I have brought you courage."

No one had ever spoken to me about my soul, but comments about my body I understood well enough. I laughed harshly. "Why would an . . . an angel speak to me about freedom, I who will be wed lifelong to my lord the king?"

"The time of your escape is at hand, and I have been sent to guide you on your path."

"You may be an angel, but you speak nonsense. Everyone knows that rebellion is not sacred, not even among the Jews. Slaves who escape are punished, and servants who disobey their masters must pay the price." Suddenly, I could remember the punishments visited upon me when I at first refused to marry the king. These were memories I had worked long and hard to erase. I did not understand why these thoughts had returned to plague me.

"I have come to issue you a challenge," he insisted, unruffled by my discomposure. "A way to restore the self-respect that has been lost to you. A way to become more than a vain consort to a demanding king. A way to win your freedom, perhaps your happiness."

Gabriel's words, although they resembled the blandishments of many courtiers I had encountered, fired old, charred hopes in my mind. When I was young, I had dreamed of someone who would wait for my love, who would give me an eternal opportunity to give myself. It was a romantic hope, and I had discarded it at a very early age, knowing that such dreams were not open to a woman in my position, or indeed to most women. Instead, the lover who possessed me was thoughtless, with no feelings for me other than a dull interest in my beauty and a keen one in my father's wealth. I was forced to admit that I would rather have no one at all. I had hoped to free myself from my bodily desires; it had not occurred to me to hope for freedom from my king. I might have wanted his affections if he had sought mine; what was forced from me could not root itself within me, not in many years of marriage, not in a lifetime.

I discovered abruptly that I had been speaking my thoughts aloud to the first sympathetic ear I had encountered. Gabriel listened quietly, intently, with all of himself. Shocked at my divulgence, I nevertheless wondered how anyone could listen like that amid the noise of the world, and wished I could listen so.

"You remind me so of the maiden Istehar," he said.

I am no maiden, I thought. This, certainly, is flattery, and his listening is a sham. Or, perhaps, all women remind him of Istehar. Do angels have lovers? "Istehar?" I inquired idly.

"May I tell you a story?"

"I adore stories," I replied dryly. "Tell away."

"In the days just after the creation of the world, certain angels, others among my kind, lusted after human women and pursued them. One such angel desired the mortal woman Istehar. The angel demanded that she bare herself to him and lie with him. She agreed, but she demanded a price—that he teach her the Name of God, which, when he uttered it, caused him to rise up to heaven, and that mortals do not know."

"Clever girl, to derive profit from her misfortune. And she made use of it for some sorcery or revenge, after he lay with her?" In spite of myself, I was interested in the outcome of the story.

"He never lay with her at all. Before he could touch her, she uttered the divine Name he had taught her and flew away to the heavens, where she was rewarded for her pure heart with transformation into a star. One can see her shining among the Pleiades to this day."

"A charming tale. Regrettably, in Persia a mortal woman cannot fly away from her admirers."

"But she can face and fight those who would coerce her. With courage, you can become free from those who enslave you."

I had never thought of myself as a slave, but I was more moved by the story of Istehar than I cared to admit. I had often wished for a way to escape from the king, when his attentions grew persistent, drunken, and violent, a way to steer my own fate. Yet Gabriel's offer of freedom seemed preposterous to me, a child's notion, easily dispelled by the realities of life. "Women do not fight," I pointed out. "They are dependent upon men for safety." I thought of my mother, who when my father was away, always waited eagerly for his return. Unlike myself, who felt used by him as well as loved, she cherished him steadfastly. He, for his part, adored her and kept her from any trouble. I had often envied her his kindness and respect.

"And do men always make a woman safe?"

It was a good question. I did not know how to answer. When the king's men came for me, my father had not heeded my cries.

"Are you not a man who is protecting me?" I inquired flirtatiously, seeking to deflect the question.

"I am not a man at all. I am the symbol of what all people might become. It is your need to see me as a man that causes me to appear as one."

"Why do you, an angel of God, question the way things are between people."

"Permit me to tell you a story."

"Of course."

Gabriel sat cross-legged on the floor of the flower-filled chamber and began, "I once was present in two evil cities, which I had been commanded to destroy. In these cities, Sodom and Gomorrah by name, no one was allowed to help another, under penalty of death. Citizens threw stones at strangers and robbed and deceived everyone they encountered. The people of the city were so wicked that they once cruelly murdered a young woman, Palotit, because she gave food to a hungry beggar. Because of evil like this, God determined that the city should be put to the fire. Not even the righteous Abraham could dissuade him from this course of action.

"When I arrived there, I entered the house of a certain man, Lot the nephew of Abraham, Palotit's father. I came there in order to save his life, for his family was the only one in the city not wholly evil. When I arrived in his house, he sought to protect me, his honored guest, from the angry mob gathered outside, which desired to abuse and violate me, a stranger among them. Lot, the righteous man of Sodom, offered his two youngest daughters to the crowd instead of me. He heeded neither my protests nor the cries of his wife, Idit.

"I pulled him back into the house and insisted that he and his family leave Sodom right away. His older daughters, corrupted by the city, refused to leave. The younger ones followed in silence. I cautioned them not to look back. Later, as I led them from the city, Idit looked back toward Sodom, unable to leave two of her offspring in the city where her eldest child had been murdered, and equally unable to follow the man who had offered up her daughters to a destructive mob. I think, also, that she could not face those young girls, whom she had not been able to protect. Out of pity, God turned her into a pillar of salt, and Lot neither mourned for her nor prayed on her behalf. His daughters, their minds wounded, later experienced incest with their father, suffering from the fear that there were no more men to marry and care for them."

Gabriel seemed strange to me then, a bitter angel, a sharp note beautiful in its discordancy. "Those children did not understand. There were men in abundance. The difficulty was that there was no justice.

And throughout the history of the world, justice has been hard to find. Sodom was burned, but in Israel during the time of the Judges, a Levite offered his concubine to an angry crowd in the same fashion in which Lot offered his daughters. And I was not there to save her."

"And justice is the cause you offer me," I whispered softly. "But what weapon could I use to advance such a cause? It is wrong for me to dishonor myself in front of the king's court"—suddenly I believed this—"but how can I defy the king? I am like Lot's wife. If I disobey, I will be destroyed."

Gabriel drew forth a mighty scythe from the sheath hanging from his belt. The curved form seemed to grow as it was revealed to the daylight. "My weapon, this scythe, is as old as the world itself. I formed it during the first days of Creation for my battle with Sennacherib. It is the weapon of just strength, of righteous anger." Gabriel ran his shining hand along the blade, impossibly sharp, an edge of darkness.

"The weapon which belongs to you is even older," he said, "for it begins with the spoken word. "'In the beginning . . . ,' the start of the Holy Scripture, is simply the beginning of all that might be said. What would you say, if you had the voice?"

"What would I say? That my husband is a lout? That I am tired of glorifying my servitude? That I wish to belong, at last, to no one?" I threw up my hands. "These words are useless. They have no substance. They cannot be heard by anyone but myself."

"They will be heard. The king will not resist you. He will hate your words, but he will remember them. Everyone will remember them, for in the scroll that I will soon deliver, your words will be recorded for all time."

I eyed the scroll at his waist, which appeared blank. I had never hoped to be remembered by anyone but a few cranky gossips, and Gabriel's words filled me with an odd sensation. Suddenly, I was no longer lonely. I had never known that I was afflicted with loneliness, but indeed that was the pain I had hoped to address with my books. Feelings of anticipation and fulfillment suffused me, and my gratitude was boundless, but sharpened by my sudden fear that Gabriel's words might not come true.

"To whom will you deliver this scroll?" I asked abruptly.

"To Mordechai the Jew, who refuses to bow down before Haman, the evil advisor of the king."

I had met Haman a few times but knew him mostly by reputation; he had a tremendous ego and an appetite for cruelty. I stayed away from his wife, Zeresh, whose greed and meanness of spirit made her a dangerous opponent. "He must be brave who does not bow down before the strength of a powerful man."

Gabriel smiled at me. "I think you, also, will refuse to bow down." His faith in me warmed me. I found that I was even capable of thinking of others beside myself.

"And who will be afflicted with my husband's affections, should I fall in with your plan of rebellion and refuse him?"

Gabriel sighed, if angels can sigh. "Esther is her name. She has the gift of faith. She is pious, virtuous, courageous, and beautiful. She is destined to become queen in your place and save her people, the Jews, from destruction."

"And is this the cause in which you enlist me? I know the Jews only from books."

Gabriel smiled. "The Jews know themselves from books. And the cause in which I enlist you is justice."

"And, in justice's name, I should refuse my husband the right to show my nakedness to his drunken friends. It is enough that he has violated me in private. He should not offer me to a mob."

"Yes," Gabriel almost sang, rising to his feet in some private moment of joy and triumph.

"He will reject me forever." I stated bleakly. "I will no longer be queen, and my father will humiliate me for my failure."

"Yes," Gabriel acknowledged. His gaze did not waver. "But your soul will be whole again."

"I accept your challenge," I declared, with a show of bravery I did not entirely feel. "But I place a condition on my acceptance."

Gabriel frowned but remained silent.

"Teach me the divine Name," I demanded. "If you truly have faith in me, as you have in this Esther, let me know what the angels know. Leave something inside me beside my beauty, which, when I use my voice against my husband, will no longer be my shield."

For the first time, Gabriel looked worried. "Only one Divine appellation has been entrusted to me. If I give the Name to you," he stammered, "there will be no Name for the Book of Esther."

"Esther has her piety, her virtue, and her people," I snapped. "I have none of those things." Then, imagining Esther as a friend instead of a rival, I softened my words. "You say she has the gift of faith. From her youth she found God inside herself. When I look inward I see nothing there but a vain and bitter woman. Istehar, Palotit, Idit, these women you have paraded in front of me as examples, they had faith to strengthen them. I have nothing except desperation, and your word."

"Faith is acquired over many years," Gabriel told me sternly.

"I don't have many years. I only have a few minutes, and I need to make them count. You are asking me to give up everything I know. You must give up something you know as well."

For the first time in my life, I had made a decision I would abide by, no matter what happened. Gabriel looked at me for a long time.

Then he leaned near me, and I felt the brush of wings, heard the faint sound of a breath, and on my mouth was the feeling of a kiss, although nothing had touched me. Then Gabriel was gone, and only a perfect, closed, rosebud remained in the place where he had been.

I had given my word to an angel, and I would keep my promise. It was to be my last act as queen, and I made it a magnificent one. I strode out of the chamber, refusing to look back, for now that I had fulfilled Gabriel's wish I was sure I had seen him for the last time. I found my way out of the servant's halls into the royal chambers, which seemed so much smaller than they had the day before. I summoned the herald who waited there ready to conduct me to the king's banquet, where I was supposed to strip naked and display myself. The idea that I would do this thing seemed so much more ridiculous than it had when I first heard it that I wondered if I were the same person.

Strangely, the courtier did not seem impatient, and I realized, as at the end of a dream, that almost no time had passed since I had fled to the simple gardener's room. I drew myself up to the impossible height and beauty of a woman wearing a crown, the height and beauty I no longer wanted. I brushed past the messenger and entered the royal banquet hall, where the king sat with his wine-soaked guests. The herald hastily announced me. Everyone turned to watch me enter.

The king frowned mightily when he saw that I was clothed. I was not afraid of him. Inside myself I held a holy secret, and the knowledge that an angel trusted me. What was inside was unpronounceable, yet I found my voice. I spoke directly to my husband.

"I refuse to be paraded in front of your revelers like an exotic trained beast. I am your wife, and even if I were only your milkmaid, I would be worthy of more respect than you have shown me. Your request is obscene, and furthermore, you are a drunken boor. I will not be commanded by you, and no one who believes in justice should obey you or heed your words." Leaving my royal spouse gaping and the entire court in stunned silence, I swept out of the hall in a wave of peacock-colored robes, the robes I had donned for my magnificent banquet. They seemed heavy to me now, the remains of a beauty I must shed so that my soul might survive. No man would protect me now, and if I did not escape, I might be executed for my disobedience. Although I knew I should pack a few belongings and find a way out of Shushan, I could not imagine anywhere on earth that would tolerate a woman such as I had become. As I quickly passed from room to room, somehow I was drawn to the chamber where I had experienced the first real friendship of my life. The act of speaking had saved me from a meaningless existence, and somehow I knew that I needed to speak again, even if only to a memory.

I was certain that when I reached the earth-colored room with its vases of humble wildflowers and modest sprays of roses, no angel would appear, for my messenger had surely gone to deliver his scroll to Mordechai. To my joy, when I arrived in the small chamber, a scroll-less Gabriel regarded me, first in satisfaction, seeing a new, purposeful light in my face, then in concern. "Vashti, a world has closed to you, but many have opened. Where will you go now?" And at that moment I knew.

In the court of Persia, no one survives who cannot learn from a good story. Like Istehar, I rose to the heavens—the heavens of the Jews, for how could I resist a paradise of books? Gabriel, chiding and laughing, rose golden-hearted after me. I think he was glad. I *know* he was glad, for in that moment we were completely open to each other. Gaining my freedom, I had revealed myself at last. Do angels have lovers? Truly I cannot say, for in the upper worlds no being has gender or even form. I will say this: no mortal loved me as well as Gabriel, who showed me the beauty of my soul.

In this paradise of trees and books, there are no servants, for none need be masters. There is only one Ruler, and that Rule is better than any I have ever known. Standing before the divine throne, I would have shivered, thinking myself once again in the court of my tyrant husband, but the incorporeal do not shiver, and in any case, the voice I perceived was not wanton and loud, but still and small as the breath of a hummingbird. There was no test of beauty. I, Vashti, was welcome.

I soon embarked upon my second friendship, with Enoch the heavenly chronicler. He, like me, came here without dying. It was he who first called me Ofanniel, an angel's name. Though surely I was no angel in my time on earth, the name delights: "wheel of God," a reminder that in an hour, everything can change. Now I, like Gabriel, am a symbol of what all people might be.

What I desired most was to give of myself, and Gabriel assigned me the task of guiding the moon. The work is intricate, complicated, requiring a sure hand and keen eye, and yet is suited to me, who wove my way through the king's court with grace and skill. I feel an affinity with the moon, keeper of the months, watcher of time, emblem of the renewal of life, and metaphor for the Shekhinah, God's divine, queenly presence. She, like me, reveals Herself only in Her own time.

As we conclude, a blessing . . .

Leah's Blessing—A Midrash
by Jill Hammer

Whom might we see if we could watch those whose path through history was hidden? What might we hear if we could listen across time to those who were silent? What blessing might we receive from those who blessed outside the holy text, if we knew how to ask for it?

Three generations of women:

LEAH: matriarch, ancestress of priests, prophets, kings, and the Messiah, wife of Jacob, and mother of Dinah. One legend has it that her eyes were weak from constant study. Rashi tells us that Leah was a woman who "went out," who was forthright and bold. She was estranged from both sister and husband, and we know little of her private life. The mystics identify Leah with the upper world, realm of hidden knowledge, divine understanding, and creative power. Leah died in Canaan and was buried in Machpelah, with the patriarchs, and with the matriarchs Rivka and Sarah, her aunt and great-grand-aunt. This midrash takes place at the time of her death.

DINAH: daughter of Leah, survivor of rape at the hands of Shechem, who was avenged by her brothers with a great massacre. Of her Rashi says: "Like mother, like daughter," for she too was one who "went out." Her name means "judgment"; she is a woman alone in the desert. One legend of her tells that she became Job's wife, but we know little of what happened to her in later life. How she forged a new identity out of trauma is unknown. This midrash takes place in Dinah's early adulthood.

SERACH: daughter of Asher, granddaughter of Jacob and Zilpah, and two generations removed from Leah the matriarch. Only her name is

173

mentioned in the Scriptures—"and Serach their sister" (Genesis 46:17). Two midrashim tell us something of her life. Serach was the one to tell Jacob that Joseph was alive. While Jacob's sons feared that the news might shock and kill their father, Serach played to him upon the harp and sang him the news, thus comforting him. She lived through slavery in Egypt: while the rest of Israel prepared for the Exodus, she showed Moses the place where Joseph had been buried, that his bones might be carried up out of Egypt. Her devotion to her family is legendary. This midrash takes place in Serach's early adolescence.

Leah's Blessing

LEAH: Dinah, are you there?

DINAH: I am here with you, mother.

LEAH: Dinah, where are your brothers?

DINAH: They have left the tent. They are going to comfort my father.

LEAH: Where is Serach?

SERACH: Here I am, within the tent.

LEAH: What I am about to say is for both of you. The Eternal has given the mothers of our people the gift of prophecy so that they will know what will happen to their children—so that they will know what to do to pass the tradition on to the next generation. Sarah sent Ishmael and Hagar into the desert so that God's promise would continue through Isaac. Rebekah knew that Jacob was meant to inherit the covenant and helped him to obtain his father's blessing. This knowledge was a heavy gift for them, and now it is a heavy gift for me.

Dinah, I am going the way of all the earth. My life has been long and difficult. I left my mother's house long ago. I do not share your father's tent, and now your brothers are with your father. My sister Rachel is buried on the road to Ephrath. I bore six sons, but only one daughter, and it is to you I offer my final blessing.

Serach, in all Jacob's multitude of grandchildren the name of only one granddaughter has been recorded. That name is yours. You should know that in the writings of our people your mother will have no name, and your grandmother Zilpah will be known only as Jacob's concubine. In spite of this, you are the next generation of the women of our people. I, Leah, adopt you. I will be your mother along with the nameless woman who bore you. I offer my words to you so that you may carry them with you when I am gone.

We will not always live as nomads in the land of Canaan. The children of Serach's generation will be slaves in Egypt. A long sojourn has been decreed for your brothers.

SERACH: Our brothers? Grandmother, will we too not go down to Egypt?

LEAH: You will not be left behind. The women will accompany the men into that dark place. But the sojourn of your daughters will be longer than the time spent in Egypt. After the revelation of the Law, even after the entrance of the nation into the land that was promised, your fullness will not be reached.

With my husband, Jacob, and my sister Rachel, I have brought forth and guided this beloved people for most of my life. In my tent I taught you that you have responsibility to the Eternal: no more, no less, than your brothers. With the help of the Almighty, I have assumed that responsibility and been a leader to all the people in our camp. That work will be all but forgotten. Before the day when I am acknowledged as equal to your father, thousands of years will pass.

DINAH: Mother, you speak of thousands of years. Surely you are speaking of the future of a great nation.

LEAH: Dinah, twelve tribes will be established among our people. They will dwell in this holy land, and in all places, and among them will be priests and judges and prophets of the Eternal. Indeed, we will be a great nation.

DINAH: Twelve tribes will be established upon the land, one for each of Jacob's sons. Then I am not counted among Jacob's children.

LEAH: It is a bitter thing I tell you, Dinah. Exclusion is painful, I know, but it can also be a source of valuable experience. Use that experience to transmit the teaching I am about to give you.

Your brothers have much to learn. They have confessed to me a terrible crime against Joseph—a crime they committed because they feared his power. The nature of humankind is to be fearful of the uncontrollable, so other nations will seek to control us—and men will seek to control women. The tradition will fear in you those things that are powerful.

In spite of this, you must understand that you are part of what makes our people strong. I am asking of you what your father expects of your brothers without asking, for unless you all agree to this, your father and I will fail in our charge. Renew the covenant that was made with Abraham and Sarah: with all its frailties, it contains within it the presence of the Eternal. It is a long way to redemption, but I know that you will carry the covenant forward until that time. I ask this of you, Dinah, and of you, Serach.

SERACH: Grandmother, what will the covenant demand of us? When we become a nation, what will be required of our daughters?

LEAH: In that time, Serach, women will be valued as helpmates, teaching the children, supporting and completing the work of man. It may be long before your brothers understand that you have your own journey to make. Nevertheless, some women of our people will arise as leaders. One of my great-granddaughters will dance a dance at the shore of the Red Sea that our people will never forget, and another of my descendants will become a judge of our people, and will sing a song of victory that is set forth for all time in the holy books.

DINAH: Mother, you comfort me. We will be permitted to sing, then, under the laws that our people will make?

LEAH: No. You will not always be permitted to sing. In time to come, the teachers of our people will judge a woman's voice too sensual for men to hear.

DINAH: Mother, my voice is precious to me. I cannot do what you ask of me.

LEAH: Dinah, what we do now is of great importance. It is our task to carry out this work. Later generations of Israel will model their behavior on ours, and will learn from what we have done. They will remember the names of the patriarchs in the most sacred of their prayers.

DINAH: But not yours.

LEAH: Someday perhaps they will remember my name was well. That day will be the reward of work that only you can do, and in this, your voice is not forbidden, but required. You must see that the women of our people are strong within, knowing themselves and their hopes and dreams. Their dedication to the covenant must equal that of the men.

The sons and daughters of Israel cannot survive independently. Dinah, my daughter, you must be reconciled.

DINAH: Do you think I wish to be a support to men—their possession, their fruitful property, to make them prosper at my expense? Was I not raped by a man who thought I belonged to him? After that horror, my brothers could think only of their own need for vengeance—their own violated honor! What about my pain? What about my violated youth? How can you ask me to teach my daughters to support this tradition? How can you ask me to subordinate myself to the covenant of our people when the teachings based on that covenant will barely acknowledge my existence?

LEAH: You are no one's possession, and yet you are wanted by the Eternal, who created you. The Almighty made this covenant with your great-grandfather and great-grandmother long before you were born. Now they are gone, and your father and I, who kept that contract, are old, but the covenant must continue in you. That covenant is the record of our conversation with the Divine. If that conversation were to end, we would surely lose our way.

DINAH: Do you keep this covenant out of loyalty to my father? Was he so kind to you? He has not been as faithful to you as you have been to him! Judah, Reuben, all of them have treated women as objects for their gratification. What claim do all these men have on me, who never asked me what I wanted? I will walk my own path, and not one of their choosing!

LEAH: My beloved child, love is a very complicated thing, as I have discovered, these long years with Jacob, and as many women of our people will discover in generations to come. But my love for your father by itself would not be enough for me to ask this thing. We have begun something beautiful in this wilderness. If it is continued, it will provide spiritual guidance for our descendants for many ages, in many places. No matter how much they change, this teaching will have wisdom to share with them. If you make this your path, you will bring new hope into the world, and the potential for peace. Yet it cannot survive if you do not give it your strength.

DINAH: I do not want my strength to be used against me. If they need me, let them come me on my own terms.

LEAH: They are not yet ready to do that.

DINAH: This is a stubborn people, as well you know. Perhaps my brothers will never be ready. Perhaps my sisters will lose their readiness as well. I cannot face that possibility.

LEAH: The Eternal will give you courage, and you must make them ready.

DINAH: Mother, you have been my teacher and comforter all my life. For your sake, I will give thought to what you have said.

LEAH: Serach, you are younger than your father's sister, but I have seen how loving is your devotion to our family. Are you ready to accept this burden in my place?

SERACH: Grandmother Leah, I will sustain the covenant. I am prepared to sacrifice for the common good. I have loved my father, and I know that his plan for our people is a good one. I have faith in my uncles and brothers, and I have faith that someday I shall build a strong family of my own. I will be proud to raise children, for children are our most precious resource. If women perform the work of passing the tradition to the next generation, of sanctifying the home and bringing joy and courage to daily work and their families, they will have honor always among our people. I am more than content with that.

LEAH: Serach, your willingness is praiseworthy, but like your sister, you do not understand everything that I have said. You cannot raise children if you have no sense of what they must be taught. Love is not the only thing you will need on this journey, and children cannot look to you for fullness if you are an empty vessel. It is a good thing to marry in joy and teach children. In time to come, there will be more than that for you to do, for you must strive for life, and it is change that guards life.

SERACH: Having seen the wars of the desert, I know that peace is the most precious gift. I want to build peace, not uproot it, and change can bring struggle and strife. What could I change that would increase the virtue of our people?

LEAH: Our teachers will praise women for modesty and charity such as yours, and the virtuous among our daughters will sustain our people throughout the generations. But do not forget, Serach, that virtue, though it provides discipline, is not meant to be a cage, and stagnation brings injustice, not peace. Do not be kept in ignorance in virtue's name, or ignorance will divide you from your goals. Most of all, do not let the fearful among our people separate you from the holy texts, for those texts will become the life of our people, and it is those texts that you must teach. Without study, your understanding will be little and fleeting.

Serach, if you will teach the children, teach your daughters to know themselves. Repeat the tale of the striving of their souls. Make it a song that passes timelessly through the generations, quiet as a lullaby yet loud as the shofar blast, so that when my daughters need a fountain of inner strength and grace, it will be there, no matter how late they seek it.

SERACH: Grandmother, you speak of timelessness, and yet I know that much will change in the coming years. I have known only the desert and its customs. I am afraid of the days that are ahead, for they are not what I have known.

LEAH: My child, do not be frightened of change. Our people must learn to adapt to new times and places. That will always be true. Preserve the tradition, and be ready to defend it from those who would from malice or thoughtlessness destroy it, but always be ready to add to it for the good. Especially be ready to distill within it your heart, for without our hearts within it the tradition is a lifeless thing.

SERACH: Grandmother, I think I understand. I know now that my voice is precious.

LEAH: Your voice will grow stronger and more beautiful with time.

Dinah, in all this time you have not spoken. Do not let the tradition become lifeless for lack of your words.

DINAH: How shall I place my heart within a tradition that has no place for me? Mother, you have not answered me, and I cannot contain my grief. Why have I no inheritance among my brothers? Each one of them will become head of a tribe, each one will gain a portion in the land which is promised. Bless me also with a portion, and I will inherit the covenant as you have said.

LEAH: Dinah, I can give you only one answer. Let my spirit be your inheritance. It is all I have to give you. I have no land to divide into portions for my daughters, nor can I make them ruler of tribes, but I can give them my spirit. I can give the wisdom of an old woman, the courage of a wanderer in the desert, and a mother's love. I will always be with you.

What words can I use to explain to you the beauty of this faith that is being born? How can I show you the poetry of prayer that is to come, or the fire of prophecy, or the chanting of the Law in the school, in the home? Can I describe for you the psalms of the Levites, the hope created under the marriage canopy, the joy of the festivals, or the peace of the Sabbath? Dinah, Serach, without you none of this can come to be. Half a people is no people. I am making you a promise that there will come a time when you will share all of this equally with your brothers. But you and your daughters are the ones who must keep that promise.

Tell your brothers! My time has come. It is you who must tell them. They cannot create a woman's way of knowing within their philosophy, their mysticism, and expect it to substitute for our being. You must tell them that, from generation to generation, until they hear you. This is all the heritage I have to offer you.

DINAH: Mother, you have given us a great gift. Your spirit will be all that we need to forge the link between the tradition and our hearts. Now I am willing to make you this promise: The covenant will be renewed with my life.

SERACH: Grandmother, we will keep your trust. Neither fear nor love will cause us to break our promise to you.

LEAH: Let the Eternal, who is present with us, be praised, and may you be given strength to do as you have promised. Come close to me, children, and let me give you my final blessing.

My kind, gentle Serach, there is much that is good in the world, but there is much that is evil. I know that the people Israel will benefit from your selfless concern for their welfare. As a parting gift, I ask you: Learn to be angry. If you never speak of your needs, others will claim they know what is best for you. Our people will need your clear voice. Do not be silent.

My passionate, proud Dinah, I ask you: Do not separate yourself from your people. They need your strength and your courage, your wisdom and your passion—and your love. Do not abandon the tradition of your fathers when it becomes too heavy for you. Remember that it is my tradition as well—the tradition of your mother—and strive to make it yours.

My beloved daughters, I was never reconciled with my sister

Rachel—her death came too quickly, before I could truly speak to her. Do not make the same mistake with your sisters and daughters. Be loving to one another, for there is strength in community, and wisdom in consultation, and there will be peace for you in the company of women.

My daughters, be strong and of good courage, and do all that I have asked you to do in the name of the Eternal. Now, call your father, Jacob, for I must speak with him about the future that belongs to all of our children. We are birthing this people, he and I together.

"And Leah died, and was buried in the cave of Machpelah." These words are not written in Genesis, yet they are true and enduring. May we be as Sarah, Rebekah, Rachel, and Leah, and may we be blessed to hear the voices of our mothers. Amen, selah.

REFERENCES

Bach, Alice, and Exum, J. Cheryl. *Miriam's Well.* New York: Delacorte Press, 1991.

Bialik, Hayim Nahman, and Ravnitzky, Yehoshua Hana, eds. *The Book of Legends.* Trans. William G. Braude. New York: Schocken Books, 1992.

Boyarin, Daniel. *Intertextuality and the Reading of Midrash.* Bloomington: Indiana University Press, 1990.

Braude, William G. *The Midrash on Psalms.* Trans. William G. Braude. New Haven, CT: Yale University Press, 1959.

Bronner, Leila Leah. *From Eve to Esther.* Louisville, KY: Westminster John Knox Press, 1994.

Buchmann, Christina, and Spiegel, Celina, eds. *Out of the Garden.* New York: Fawcett Columbine, 1994.

Buttrick, George Arthur, et al., eds. *The Interpreter's Dictionary of the Bible.* New York: Abingdon Press, 1962.

Eichler, Barry L., and Tigay, Jeffrey H., eds. *Studies in Midrash and Related Literature.* Philadelphia: Jewish Publication Society, 1988.

Epstein, I., et al., ed. and trans. *The Babylonian Talmud.* London: Soncino Press, 1935–1952.

Freedman, H., and Simon, Maurice, et al., eds. and trans., *The Midrash.* London: Soncino Press, 1951.

Frymer-Kensky, Tikva. *In the Wake of the Goddess.* New York: Free Press, 1992.

Ginzberg, Louis. *The Legends of the Jews.* Philadelphia: Jewish Publication Society, 1942–1947.

Goodrick, Edward W., and Kohlenberger, John R. III, eds. *The NIV Exhaustive Concordance.* Grand Rapids, MI: Zondervan Publishing House, 1990.

Gottlieb, Lynn. *She Who Dwells Within.* San Francisco, CA: HarperSan-
Francisco, 1995.

Graetz, Naomi. *S/He Created Them.* Chapel Hill, NC: Professional Press,
1993.

Heschel, Susannah, ed. *On Being a Jewish Feminist.* New York: Schocken
Books, 1983.

Holtz, Barry W., ed. *Back to the Sources.* New York: Summit Books, 1984.

The Holy Scriptures. Tel Aviv: Sinai Publishing, 1979.

Jacobson, David C. *Modern Midrash.* Albany: State University of New
York Press, 1987.

Kates, Judith A., and Reimer, Gail Twersky, eds. *Reading Ruth.* New York:
Ballantine Books, 1994.

Koltun, Elizabeth, ed. *The Jewish Woman.* New York: Schocken Books,
1976.

Koltuv, Barbara Black. *The Book of Lilith.* York Beach, ME: Nicolas-Hays,
1986.

Mekhilta de-Rabbi Ishmael. Trans. Jacob Z. Lauterbach. Philadelphia:
Jewish Publication Society, 1949.

Meyers, Carol. *Discovering Eve.* New York: Oxford University Press,
1988.

Midrash Tanhuma. Trans. John T. Townsend. Hoboken, NJ: Ktav Publishing House, 1989.

Neusner, Jacob. *The Midrash: An Introduction.* Northvale, NJ: Jason
Aronson, 1990.

————. *A Midrash Reader.* Minneapolis, MN: Fortress Press, 1990.

Ostriker, Alicia Suskin. *The Nakedness of the Fathers: Biblical Vision and
Revisions.* New Brunswick, NJ: Rutgers University Press, 1994.

Piercy, Marge. *Mars and Her Children.* New York: Alfred A. Knopf, 1992.

Plaskow, Judith. *Standing again at Sinai.* San Francisco, CA: HarperSan-
Francisco, 1991.

Plaut, W. Gunther, ed. *The Torah: A Modern Commentary.* New York:
Union of American Hebrew Congregations, 1981.

Porton, Gary G. *Understanding Rabbinic Midrash.* Hoboken, NJ: Ktav
Publishing House, 1985.

Scherman, Nosson. *The Chumash.* Brooklyn, NY: Mesorah Publications,
1993.

Schwartz, Leo W., ed. *Great Ages and Ideas of the Jewish People*. New York: Modern Library, 1956.

Segal, Naomi. "Midrash and Feminism." *Paragraph* 13:3 (November 1992): 251–266.

Stern, David, and Mirsky, Mark, eds. *Rabbinic Fantasies*. Trans. Norman Bronznick et al. Philadelphia: Jewish Publication Society, 1990.

TaNaKH. Philadelphia: Jewish Publication Society, 1985.

Trible, Phyllis. *Texts of Terror: Literary-Feminist Readings of Biblical Narratives*. Philadelphia: Fortress Press, 1984.

Umansky, Ellen, and Ashton, Dianne, eds. *Four Centuries of Jewish Women's Spirituality*. Boston: Beacon Press, 1992.

The Zohar. Trans. Harry Sperling and Maurice Simon. Rebecca Bennet Publications, [n.d.].

Zones, Jane Sprague, ed. *Taking the Fruit: Modern Women's Tales of the Bible*. San Diego, CA: Women's Institute for Continuing Jewish Education, 1989.

CREDITS

INDEX

About the Author

Naomi Mara Hyman is a poet, midrashist, and teacher of Jewish Women's Spirituality. An advisory board member of the Institute for Contemporary Midrash, she holds a masters degree in Jewish Studies and is currently pursuing rabbinic ordination. Her work has previously appeared in *Kerem: Creative Explorations in Judaism*.